AI Consulting 101:

Building a Successful Career in Artificial Intelligence

Matu Mureithi

Table of Contents

Introduction 1
   Welcome to the World of AI Consulting 1
Part 1: Building a Strong Foundation 4
Chapter 1: Understanding AI and Its Applications 6
   1.1 What is Artificial Intelligence? 7
   1.3 Real-Life AI Use Cases in Consulting 11
   1.4 The Ethical Dimensions of AI 12
   1.5 The Future of AI and Its Potential 13
Chapter 2: Developing a Solid Technical Background 16
   2.1 Mathematics and Statistics for AI Consultants 17
   2.2 Programming Languages and Tools for AI Development 18
   2.3 Data Management and Preprocessing 19
Chapter 3: Nurturing Your Problem-Solving Skills 22
   3.2 Problem-Solving Frameworks for AI Projects 24
   3.3 Understanding Business Challenges and Goals 26
Part 2: AI Consulting Process 28
Chapter 4: Scoping AI Projects 30
   4.1 Defining Project Objectives and Scope 31
   4.2 Assessing Feasibility and Resources 32
   4.3 Risk Assessment and Mitigation Strategies 34
Chapter 5: Data Collection and Preparation 36
   5.1 Data Sourcing and Collection Techniques 37
   5.2 Data Cleaning and Preprocessing 38
   5.3 Dealing with Data Privacy and Security 40
Chapter 6: AI Model Selection and Development 42
   6.1 Understanding Various AI Models (Machine Learning, Deep Learning, NLP, etc.)4
   6.1 Evaluating Model Suitability for Specific Tasks 45
   6.3 Implementing and Fine-Tuning AI Models 46

Chapter 7: AI Model Evaluation and Validation 49
7.1 Performance Metrics for AI Models 50
7.2 Cross-Validation and Testing Techniques 52
7.3 Ensuring Model Robustness and Fairness 53

Chapter 8: Deployment and Integration 55
8.1 Integrating AI Solutions into Existing Systems 56
8.2 Handling Deployment Challenges 57
8.3 Post-Deployment Monitoring and Maintenance 59

Part 3: Mastering the Soft Skills 62

Chapter 9: Communication and Client Management 64
9.1 Effective Communication Strategies 65
9.2 Presenting Complex AI Concepts to Non-Technical Stakeholders 66
9.3 Building and Maintaining Client Relationships 68

Chapter 10: Ethical and Legal Considerations 70
10.1 Addressing Bias and Fairness in AI 71
10.2 Ensuring Ethical AI Practices 72
10.3 Navigating Legal and Regulatory Frameworks 74

Chapter 11: Staying Updated in the Dynamic AI Landscape 76
11.1 Continuous Learning and Skill Enhancement 77
11.2 Networking and Engaging in AI Communities 78
11.3 Staying Informed About Latest AI Trends 80

AI consulting project case studies: 83
Reflecting on Your Journey to Becoming an AI Consultant 85
Words of Advice from Experienced AI Consultants 86

Appendix: 88
Glossary of AI Terminology 88
Additional Resources for Further Learning 89

Dedication

To all AI Enthusiasts,

This book is dedicated to you, the visionaries, innovators, and dreamers who have embraced the transformative power of AI. Your passion and curiosity have ignited the spark that propels us into the future of AI-powered innovation. Your unwavering dedication to pushing the boundaries of what's possible inspires us to constantly strive for excellence in the realm of AI.

Through your pursuit of knowledge and the relentless pursuit of unlocking AI's true potential, you are shaping industries, revolutionizing businesses, and enriching lives. Your commitment to ethical and responsible AI development serves as a guiding light, ensuring that AI's impact on society remains positive and beneficial.

As we embark on this journey together, we celebrate your invaluable contributions to the world of AI. May this book empower you with the insights and wisdom you seek, as you continue to make remarkable strides in the AI landscape.

Here's to all AI Enthusiasts – the architects of a brighter, AI-driven future!

With utmost respect and admiration,

Matu Mureithi

AI Consulting 101

AI Consulting 101: Building a Successful Career in Artificial Intelligence

Edition Copyright © 2023 Allspark Ventures ltd.

All Rights Reserved

ISBN: 9798856027371

No part of this book may be reproduced in any form,

by photocopying or by any electronic or mechanical means,

including information storage or retrieval systems,

without permission in writing from both the copyright

owner and the publisher of this book.

First Published Date 4-08-2023
Allspark Ventures ltd

Introduction

An AI Consultant is a highly specialized professional who collaborates with organizations to identify AI opportunities, design tailored AI solutions, and guide the seamless integration of AI technologies. As industries evolve at an unprecedented pace, the significance of AI Consultants becomes paramount, shaping the trajectory of businesses, and unlocking the full potential of AI-powered innovation.

Welcome to the World of AI Consulting

Artificial Intelligence (AI) has emerged as one of the most transformative technologies of the modern era, revolutionizing industries, businesses, and societies at an unprecedented pace. As AI continues to permeate every aspect of our lives, organizations worldwide are seeking to harness its potential to gain a competitive edge and drive innovation. This insatiable demand for AI expertise has given rise to a thriving field known as AI consulting, where skilled professionals help businesses navigate the complex landscape of AI implementation.

If you have ever been captivated by the possibilities of AI, envisioning a future where intelligent machines aid in decision-making, automate repetitive tasks, and elevate human potential, then embarking on a journey to become an AI consultant might be the path for you.

This book, "AI Consulting 101," is designed to guide you through the intricacies of mastering artificial intelligence in the consulting world. Whether you are an aspiring data scientist, a business strategist, or an industry expert, this comprehensive guide will equip you with the knowledge, skills, and confidence needed to thrive in the exciting domain of AI consulting.

In the chapters that follow, we will take you through a step-by-step process, beginning with laying a robust foundation in AI and building your technical prowess. We will explore the methodologies for scoping AI projects, collecting and preparing data, and selecting appropriate AI models for specific business challenges. As you progress, you will learn how to evaluate, validate, deploy, and integrate AI solutions effectively.

But becoming an AI consultant isn't just about understanding algorithms and models. It requires a unique blend of technical proficiency and soft skills. You will discover the importance of honing your problem-solving abilities, communicating complex ideas to diverse audiences, and managing client relationships with finesse.

Moreover, we will delve into the ethical considerations surrounding AI and the responsibility of AI consultants in shaping a fair and inclusive future.

As with any rapidly evolving field, staying current in the dynamic AI landscape is essential. We will offer insights into continuous learning, networking with industry professionals, and navigating the ever-changing realm of AI trends.

Throughout this book, you will encounter real-world case studies, practical examples, and expert advice from seasoned AI consultants. Their experiences will shed light on the challenges and rewards of the profession, providing you with valuable lessons and inspiring anecdotes to fuel your own journey.

So, whether you aspire to guide Fortune 500 companies in adopting AI solutions, work with startups to innovate disruptive technologies, or collaborate with governmental organizations to address societal challenges, "AI Consulting 101" will serve as your compass, leading you toward a rewarding and impactful career in AI consulting.

Let us begin this exciting expedition into the realm of AI consulting, where the convergence of human ingenuity and artificial intelligence is reshaping the world, one algorithm at a time.

Embrace the possibilities, and let's chart a course together to transform your aspirations into reality.

Why AI Consulting Matters

In today's fast-paced and hyper-competitive business landscape, AI consulting has emerged as a critical catalyst for success. As companies grapple with the complexities of the digital age, the adoption of AI has become not just a strategic advantage but a necessity to thrive and innovate. AI consulting matters, and here's why:

a) **Harnessing the Power of Data:** Data has become the lifeblood of modern enterprises, and AI is the key to unlocking its true potential. AI algorithms can analyze vast datasets with incredible speed and accuracy, extracting valuable insights that would be impossible to uncover manually. Through AI consulting, organizations can turn raw data into actionable knowledge, fueling data-driven decision-making and gaining a competitive edge.

b) **Accelerating Innovation:** In a world where innovation drives progress, AI stands at the forefront of groundbreaking discoveries. AI technologies like machine learning and natural language processing have paved the way for revolutionary advancements in various fields. AI consulting empowers businesses to identify and implement these innovations effectively, staying ahead of the curve and redefining the boundaries of what's possible.

c) **Enhancing Customer Experience:** Personalization and seamless interactions are no longer optional; they are customer expectations. AI enables businesses to deliver highly personalized experiences, from targeted marketing campaigns to intelligent customer support. By leveraging AI consulting, organizations can elevate their customer experience, fostering loyalty and building lasting relationships.

d) **Optimizing Operations and Efficiency:** In an era where efficiency is paramount, AI streamlines operations across the board. AI-driven automation reduces manual work, minimizes errors, and accelerates processes, leading to increased productivity and cost savings. AI consulting helps organizations identify areas where automation can be most beneficial and implements solutions that optimize efficiency.

e) **Predictive Insights and Forecasting:** AI's ability to analyze historical data and identify patterns allows businesses to make informed predictions and forecasts. From sales projections and demand forecasting to inventory management and risk analysis, AI consulting equips organizations with powerful predictive capabilities, enabling them to make better decisions and mitigate potential risks.

f) **Unleashing Creativity and Innovation:** Contrary to the fear that AI may replace human creativity, AI can be a powerful tool to augment human creativity and innovation. AI consultants work with teams to identify ways AI can enhance and amplify creative processes, freeing up valuable human resources to focus on higher-level tasks that require human ingenuity.

g) **Tackling Complex Challenges:** Businesses today face increasingly complex challenges that demand sophisticated solutions. AI consulting brings together a diverse set of skills and expertise to address these challenges head-on. From designing AI-driven supply chain optimization to implementing predictive maintenance in manufacturing, AI consultants tackle multifaceted problems with ingenuity and precision.

h) **Future-Proofing Organizations:** As AI continues to evolve, its integration becomes essential for the long-term viability of organizations. Through AI consulting, businesses can lay a solid foundation for the future, ensuring that they remain adaptable and resilient in the face of technological disruptions.

Conclusion: AI consulting matters because it empowers businesses to leverage the potential of AI, unlocking new possibilities, driving innovation, and fostering sustainable growth. With the guidance and expertise of AI consultants, organizations can navigate the complexities of the AI landscape and harness its transformative power to stay ahead in a rapidly changing world.

Part 1: Building a Strong Foundation

Chapter 1: Understanding AI and Its Applications

In this introductory chapter, we delve into the fundamental concepts of Artificial Intelligence (AI) and explore its diverse applications in the real world. We demystify the essence of AI, including its history, goals, and underlying principles. Through concrete examples, we showcase how AI has already revolutionized industries such as healthcare, finance, transportation, and more. By the end of this chapter, readers will have a solid grasp of AI's potential and its significance in shaping the future of businesses and society.

Chapter 2: Developing a Solid Technical Background

A strong technical foundation is essential for aspiring AI consultants. In this chapter, we explore the core technical skills required to excel in AI consulting. We dive into the world of mathematics and statistics, unveiling the importance of concepts like linear algebra, calculus, probability, and more in AI development. Additionally, we provide insights into programming languages and tools commonly used in AI projects, such as Python, TensorFlow, and PyTorch. By the end of this chapter, readers will have a clear roadmap for enhancing their technical proficiency and setting a solid foundation for their AI consulting journey.

Chapter 3: Nurturing Your Problem-Solving Skills

AI consulting involves navigating complex challenges and devising innovative solutions. In this chapter, we focus on honing problem-solving skills essential for AI consultants. We explore critical thinking methodologies, including root cause analysis, design thinking, and systems thinking, which enable consultants to dissect complex problems and devise efficient AI-driven solutions. Moreover, we emphasize the importance of understanding the specific business context and aligning AI strategies with organizational goals. By the end of this chapter, readers will possess valuable problem-solving frameworks to tackle diverse AI projects effectively.

Part 1 Summary:

Building a strong foundation is paramount for aspiring AI consultants. Part 1 equips readers with essential knowledge and skills, from comprehending the essence of AI and its real-world applications to developing a robust technical background encompassing mathematics, statistics, and programming. The part culminates by nurturing problem-solving acumen, preparing consultants to approach AI projects strategically and creatively. With this comprehensive foundation, readers are ready to embark on the rest of their AI consulting journey, armed with the necessary tools to excel in this dynamic and impactful domain.

Chapter 1: Understanding AI and Its Applications

Artificial Intelligence (AI) is no longer just the stuff of science fiction; it has become an integral part of our daily lives and the driving force behind numerous technological advancements. In this chapter, we embark on a journey to explore the world of AI, unraveling its essence and understanding its vast array of applications.

1.1 What is Artificial Intelligence?

We begin by demystifying the concept of AI. We explore the fundamental definition of AI and its distinction from traditional programming. Readers will grasp the idea of AI as a technology that enables machines to mimic human cognitive functions, such as learning, reasoning, and problem-solving. We dive into the history of AI, tracing its roots back to the Dartmouth Workshop in 1956, and discuss the different types of AI, including narrow AI, general AI, and superintelligence.

1.2 AI's Impact on Businesses and Industries

The impact of AI on businesses and industries is profound and far-reaching. In this section, we showcase the transformative power of AI in various sectors. We highlight real-life success stories of companies that have leveraged AI to enhance customer experiences, optimize operations, and drive innovation. Examples from industries like e-commerce, healthcare, finance, manufacturing, and more illustrate how AI is reshaping the way organizations operate and thrive.

1.3 Real-Life AI Use Cases in Consulting

AI has become a strategic enabler for consulting firms worldwide. In this subsection, we delve into the specific applications of AI in the consulting realm. We explore how AI is used for data analytics, predictive modeling, market research, and decision support. We discuss how AI-driven insights empower consultants to offer data-driven strategies and recommendations to clients. Case studies and anecdotes from leading consulting firms demonstrate the real-world impact of AI in shaping business strategies and driving growth.

1.4 The Ethical Dimensions of AI

Understanding AI is not only about its capabilities but also its ethical implications. As AI continues to permeate every aspect of society, ethical considerations become paramount. We delve into the challenges surrounding AI ethics, including bias, transparency, and privacy. We discuss the importance of incorporating ethical practices in AI consulting to ensure fairness, trustworthiness, and accountability in AI solutions.

1.5 The Future of AI and Its Potential

In the final section of this chapter, we explore the future of AI and its vast potential. We discuss emerging trends in AI, such as reinforcement learning, explainable AI, and quantum computing's role in shaping the next generation of AI. We also examine the potential risks and opportunities presented by AI's continued development and how consultants can proactively address challenges and lead the way toward responsible and beneficial AI integration.

Conclusion: Chapter 1 provides a comprehensive overview of AI and its applications. Readers gain a solid understanding of what AI is, its impact on businesses and industries, and its relevance to the consulting world. By exploring real-life AI use cases, readers are inspired by the transformative potential of AI consulting. Additionally, the chapter emphasizes the importance of ethical considerations and prepares readers for the exciting future of AI, where they can play a pivotal role in shaping the responsible and impactful use of this revolutionary technology in consulting.

1.1 What is Artificial Intelligence?

Artificial Intelligence, often abbreviated as AI, is a multidisciplinary field of computer science and engineering that aims to create machines and systems with the ability to simulate human intelligence. The core idea behind AI is to develop intelligent agents that can perceive their environment, reason about it, learn from past experiences, and make decisions or take actions to achieve specific goals. The ultimate goal of AI is to create machines that can perform tasks typically requiring human intelligence, such as understanding natural language, recognizing objects, making predictions, and solving complex problems.

Key Concepts and Approaches in AI:

Machine Learning: Machine learning is a central component of AI, wherein algorithms enable systems to learn from data without being explicitly programmed. This approach involves training models on large datasets, allowing the algorithms to identify patterns and make predictions or decisions based on new, unseen data.

a) **Deep Learning:** Deep learning is a subfield of machine learning that utilizes artificial neural networks, inspired by the structure of the human brain. These networks consist of multiple layers of interconnected neurons, enabling the system to automatically learn hierarchical representations of data, making them highly effective in tasks like image recognition and natural language processing.

b) **Natural Language Processing (NLP):** NLP focuses on enabling machines to understand, interpret, and generate human language. NLP technologies power applications such as language translation, sentiment analysis, chatbots, and voice assistants.

c) **Computer Vision:** Computer vision is an AI area concerned with teaching machines to interpret and understand visual information from the world, including images and videos. Computer vision applications range from object detection and facial recognition to autonomous vehicles and medical image analysis.

d) **Robotics:** AI-driven robotics seeks to create machines capable of physically interacting with the world. These robots can perform tasks like assembly line work, autonomous exploration, and even assisting in healthcare settings.

AI Applications:

The applications of AI span across various industries and domains, transforming the way we live and work:

a) **Healthcare:** AI is used for medical image analysis, disease diagnosis, drug discovery, and personalized treatment plans.

b) **Finance:** In finance, AI powers fraud detection, algorithmic trading, credit risk assessment, and customer service chatbots.

c) **Transportation:** Self-driving cars and predictive maintenance in transportation are fueled by AI technologies.

d) **E-commerce:** AI-based recommendation systems drive personalized shopping experiences for consumers.

e) **Entertainment:** AI is behind personalized content recommendations on streaming platforms and AI-generated music and art.

f) **Manufacturing:** AI-enabled predictive maintenance and quality control optimize manufacturing processes.

g) **Education:** AI is used for intelligent tutoring systems, adaptive learning, and automating administrative tasks.

Challenges and Ethical Considerations:

While AI offers remarkable opportunities, it also poses significant challenges and ethical considerations. Bias in AI algorithms, data privacy concerns, job displacement due to automation, and the potential misuse of AI technology are areas that demand careful attention and responsible AI development.

Conclusion: Artificial Intelligence stands at the forefront of technological innovation, enabling machines to learn, reason, and make decisions like humans. Its applications are wide-ranging, transforming industries and improving various aspects of human life. However, as we continue to advance in this field, it is vital to navigate the ethical and societal implications of AI, ensuring that we use this powerful technology responsibly and for the benefit of humanity.

1.2 AI's Impact on Businesses and Industries

Artificial Intelligence (AI) is revolutionizing businesses and industries across the globe, reshaping traditional practices, and unlocking unprecedented opportunities for growth and efficiency. As AI technologies continue to advance, their impact on various sectors becomes increasingly profound, touching every aspect of operations and strategy. Here, we explore the remarkable ways AI is transforming businesses and industries.

a) **Enhanced Decision-Making:** AI empowers businesses with data-driven decision-making capabilities. By analyzing vast datasets and extracting valuable insights, AI systems enable organizations to make informed choices, identify patterns, and predict trends. From optimizing supply chain logistics to forecasting customer demand, AI-driven decisions lead to increased accuracy and efficiency.

b) **Personalized Customer Experiences:** In the age of hyper-personalization, AI plays a pivotal role in tailoring customer experiences. AI-driven recommendation systems analyze user behavior to offer personalized product and content recommendations, resulting in higher customer satisfaction, increased engagement, and ultimately, improved conversion rates.

c) **Automation and Efficiency:** AI-driven automation streamlines repetitive and mundane tasks, freeing up human resources to focus on more strategic and creative endeavors. Robotic Process Automation (RPA) automates routine tasks, while AI-powered chatbots handle customer inquiries, reducing response times and enhancing service efficiency.

d) **Predictive Analytics:** AI's predictive capabilities empower businesses to anticipate future trends and events. From predicting customer preferences to identifying maintenance needs in machinery before failure occurs, predictive analytics helps organizations stay proactive, minimizing risks, and capitalizing on opportunities.

e) **Advanced Marketing and Sales:** AI enables marketers to refine their strategies by analyzing customer behavior, sentiment, and engagement patterns. AI-driven marketing campaigns are more targeted and personalized, yielding higher returns on investment. In sales, AI assists with lead scoring, customer segmentation, and sales forecasting.

f) **Healthcare Advancements:** In the healthcare sector, AI has transformed diagnostics, drug discovery, and patient care. AI algorithms can analyze medical images, aiding in early disease detection and accurate diagnoses. Moreover, AI helps researchers sift through vast amounts of medical data to identify potential treatments and drug candidates.

g) **Financial Sector Innovation:** In finance, AI algorithms analyze market data to make rapid and accurate trading decisions. AI-driven fraud detection systems protect customers and institutions from financial scams. Additionally, AI-powered chatbots enhance customer service by providing instant support and assistance.

h) **Manufacturing Optimization:** AI has revolutionized manufacturing processes, enhancing efficiency and reducing costs. AI-driven predictive maintenance helps prevent equipment breakdowns and optimize maintenance schedules, reducing downtime and increasing productivity. AI-powered robots perform complex tasks with precision, boosting overall manufacturing capabilities.

i) **Autonomous Vehicles:** AI is a driving force behind the development of autonomous vehicles. Advanced AI technologies, such as computer vision and machine learning, enable self-driving cars to perceive their surroundings, navigate safely, and make real-time decisions on the road.

j) **Agriculture and Food Production:** AI-powered agricultural technologies improve crop yield and resource efficiency. AI-driven analysis of soil data and weather patterns optimizes irrigation and fertilization, leading to better crop health and reduced environmental impact. AI also plays a role in automating food production and quality control processes.

Conclusion:

AI's impact on businesses and industries is vast and transformative. From enabling data-driven decision-making and enhancing customer experiences to driving automation and efficiency across sectors, AI has become an indispensable tool for organizations seeking a competitive edge in the digital age. Embracing AI technologies and their responsible implementation will continue to shape the future of businesses, industries, and societies, unlocking new possibilities and driving innovation for years to come.

1.3 Real-Life AI Use Cases in Consulting

Artificial Intelligence (AI) has become an indispensable tool in the consulting world, revolutionizing the way firms provide strategic insights, data-driven recommendations, and innovative solutions to their clients. In this section, we delve into real-life AI use cases that have transformed the consulting industry and empowered consultants to deliver impactful results across diverse business challenges.

a) **Data Analytics and Business Intelligence:** AI-powered data analytics and business intelligence have become fundamental for consultants to unearth valuable insights from vast and complex datasets. Using machine learning algorithms, consultants can analyze historical data, identify trends, and predict future outcomes. This empowers businesses to make data-driven decisions, optimize processes, and gain a competitive edge. Data visualization tools powered by AI also aid consultants in presenting complex findings in a visually appealing and comprehensible manner to stakeholders.

b) **Predictive Modeling and Forecasting:** Consultants leverage AI to build predictive models that forecast business outcomes and trends. From sales forecasts to market demand predictions, AI-driven models offer invaluable insights for decision-making. Consultants use time series analysis, regression, and other machine learning techniques to create accurate and reliable predictive models, guiding clients to proactively respond to market changes and plan for the future.

c) **Market Research and Consumer Insights:** AI plays a pivotal role in market research and consumer insights, enabling consultants to gather, process, and analyze vast amounts of unstructured data from social media, online reviews, and customer feedback. Sentiment analysis and natural language processing (NLP) techniques help extract valuable insights into consumer preferences, sentiments, and behavior, guiding businesses to tailor their products and services for maximum customer satisfaction.

d) **Supply Chain Optimization:** Optimizing supply chain operations is a complex task for businesses. AI-driven optimization algorithms help consultants model and fine-tune supply chain networks to reduce costs, minimize lead times, and enhance overall efficiency. By analyzing historical data and real-time information, AI can predict demand patterns, optimize inventory levels, and identify potential risks in the supply chain.

e) **Fraud Detection and Risk Management:** Consultants use AI to identify and mitigate risks for their clients. In the financial industry, AI-driven fraud detection systems analyze transaction patterns and user behavior to flag suspicious activities in real-time, preventing fraudulent transactions. Additionally, AI helps consultants assess credit risk, detect anomalies, and strengthen risk management strategies.

f) **Customer Segmentation and Personalization:** AI enables consultants to analyze customer data and segment target audiences effectively. Personalized marketing campaigns can be designed to target specific customer segments based on their preferences, behaviors, and demographics. AI-driven recommendation systems also help businesses provide personalized content, products, and services to customers, enhancing engagement and loyalty.

g) **Process Automation and Robotic Process Automation (RPA):** Consultants leverage AI-driven automation and RPA to streamline and optimize business processes. Repetitive and rule-based tasks can be automated, reducing manual errors and freeing up human resources to focus on more strategic initiatives. RPA also helps improve process efficiency and reduces operational costs.

h) **Intelligent Virtual Assistants and Chatbots:** AI-powered chatbots and virtual assistants assist consultants in handling customer inquiries and providing 24/7 support. These AI systems use natural language processing to understand customer queries and provide relevant responses in real-time. By automating customer interactions, consultants can enhance customer service and improve overall customer experience.

Conclusion: Real-life AI use cases in consulting demonstrate the transformative impact of AI technologies across various business functions and industries. AI empowers consultants to unlock insights from data, predict market trends, optimize processes, and offer personalized solutions to clients. As AI continues to evolve, consultants will further leverage its capabilities to drive innovation, deliver value, and stay at the forefront of the ever-evolving consulting landscape.

1.4 The Ethical Dimensions of AI

Artificial Intelligence (AI) has emerged as a powerful force driving innovation and transformation across various industries. However, alongside its potential benefits, AI also raises profound ethical considerations that must be carefully addressed. In this chapter, we delve into the ethical dimensions of AI and explore the critical challenges and responsibilities that AI consultants must navigate to ensure responsible and ethical AI practices.

a) **The Moral Imperative:** As AI continues to shape our societies and impact human lives, it brings about a moral imperative for AI consultants to prioritize ethical decision-making. The development and deployment of AI solutions must align with human values, fairness, and the protection of human rights.

b) **Transparency and Explainability:** The black-box nature of certain AI models raises concerns about transparency and explainability. Ethical AI consultants understand the importance of explaining AI decisions to stakeholders, ensuring that users and impacted parties can comprehend how AI solutions arrive at specific outcomes.

c) **Bias and Fairness:** Bias in AI algorithms can perpetuate existing social inequalities and discriminatory practices. AI consultants must be vigilant in identifying and mitigating bias in data and algorithms to ensure fair and unbiased AI solutions.

d) **Data Privacy and Security:** The vast amounts of data used to train AI models raise significant data privacy and security concerns. Consultants must adhere to data protection regulations and implement robust security measures to safeguard sensitive information.

e) **Accountability and Responsibility:** As AI consultants, there is a shared responsibility to be accountable for the impact of AI solutions on individuals and society. Taking ownership of potential consequences and striving for continuous improvement is essential in maintaining ethical standards.

f) **Human-Centered Design:** An ethical AI consultant places humans at the center of AI system design. Understanding the needs and preferences of end-users helps create AI solutions that genuinely serve and benefit people.

g) **AI in Critical Domains:** AI's deployment in critical domains, such as healthcare and autonomous vehicles, demands heightened ethical scrutiny. Consultants must prioritize safety and human well-being in these contexts.

h) **AI and Employment:** AI's potential to automate tasks raises questions about its impact on the workforce. Ethical AI consultants must consider ways to promote responsible automation that complements human skills rather than replacing jobs.

i) **Governance and Regulation:** Ethical AI consultants support the development of robust governance frameworks and regulations that govern AI development, deployment, and use. Adherence to these guidelines fosters ethical practices at a broader level.

j) **Long-Term Impact:** Ethical considerations extend beyond immediate project timelines. AI consultants must contemplate the long-term consequences of AI solutions to ensure sustainability and positive societal impact.

k) **Ethics Review and Ethical Boards:** In certain AI projects, especially those involving sensitive data or critical applications, establishing ethics review processes and ethical boards can provide an additional layer of oversight and accountability.

Conclusion: Navigating the ethical dimensions of AI is an ongoing journey for AI consultants. It requires a commitment to continuous learning, an openness to discussions on complex ethical dilemmas, and a dedication to upholding ethical principles in all aspects of AI consulting. By embracing ethical considerations, AI consultants can contribute to the responsible and beneficial deployment of AI technologies, leading to a more equitable and inclusive AI-driven future.

1.5 The Future of AI and Its Potential

Artificial Intelligence (AI) has come a long way since its inception, and its future holds unprecedented potential to reshape the world as we know it. In this chapter, we explore the exciting prospects and possibilities that lie ahead in the field of AI, as well as the transformative impact it is poised to have on various industries and aspects of human life.

a) **Accelerating Innovation:** The rapid advancements in AI research and technology are accelerating the pace of innovation. AI consultants are at the forefront of this transformative journey, driving breakthroughs that were once deemed science fiction.

b) **AI as a Catalyst for Change:** AI is a catalyst for change in numerous industries, including healthcare, finance, manufacturing, education, and more. It is revolutionizing processes, optimizing operations, and unlocking new opportunities for growth.

c) **Empowering Human Potential:** AI's true potential lies in augmenting human capabilities rather than replacing them. AI consultants are at the vanguard of creating symbiotic relationships between AI technologies and human ingenuity.

d) **Autonomous Systems:** The future of AI holds the promise of autonomous systems, from self-driving cars to smart cities. AI consultants play a pivotal role in developing and implementing these systems, making our lives safer, more efficient, and sustainable.

e) **Personalization and Hyper-Personalization:** AI's ability to analyze vast amounts of data enables hyper-personalization of products and services. AI consultants are designing AI-driven solutions that cater to individual needs and preferences, elevating customer experiences to new heights.

f) **AI in Healthcare:** AI's potential in healthcare is immense, from disease diagnosis and personalized treatment plans to drug discovery and health monitoring. AI consultants contribute to cutting-edge solutions that improve patient outcomes and revolutionize healthcare delivery.

g) **AI and Sustainability:** AI is becoming a critical tool in addressing global challenges, such as climate change and resource management. AI consultants are exploring innovative applications of AI to foster sustainability and safeguard the environment.

h) **AI for Social Good:** AI has the power to address social issues and bridge gaps in society. AI consultants are involved in projects that harness AI for social good, including humanitarian efforts, disaster response, and enhancing accessibility for all.

i) **AI and Creativity:** AI's creativity and generative capabilities are evolving rapidly. AI consultants are pushing the boundaries of artistic expression, music composition, and creative content generation, enriching human culture with AI-augmented creativity

j) **The AI Job Market:** AI's transformative potential also raises questions about its impact on the job market. AI consultants are actively working on AI workforce integration and reskilling initiatives to ensure a smooth transition into the AI-powered future.

k) **Ethical Considerations:** The future of AI brings with it ethical dilemmas and societal challenges. AI consultants are at the forefront of developing frameworks for responsible AI deployment, ensuring fairness, transparency, and accountability.

l) **The Road Ahead:** The future of AI is a journey of continuous learning and adaptability. AI consultants must remain agile, embracing emerging technologies and approaches to navigate the evolving landscape effectively.

Conclusion: As AI consultants envision the future of AI, they become architects of a world that balances technological progress with ethical responsibility. By harnessing AI's potential for human-centric solutions, AI consultants can create a future that thrives on innovation, sustainability, and the betterment of human lives. The possibilities are boundless, and the future of AI is as much a story of human creativity as it is a testament to the power of intelligent machines.

Chapter 2: Developing a Solid Technical Background

In Chapter 2, we embark on a journey to build a strong technical foundation essential for aspiring AI consultants. The world of AI requires a deep understanding of mathematics, statistics, programming, and data management. This chapter equips readers with the knowledge and skills to navigate the technical aspects of AI development effectively.

2.1 Mathematics and Statistics for AI Consultants

Mathematics forms the bedrock of AI algorithms and models. In this section, we explore key mathematical concepts that underpin AI development. Topics such as linear algebra, calculus, probability, and optimization are demystified, with a focus on their relevance to AI applications. Readers will gain insight into how matrices and vectors are used in AI models, how derivatives enable optimization in machine learning, and how probability theory drives uncertainty quantification in AI predictions.

2.2 Programming Languages and Tools for AI Development

Proficiency in programming languages and AI tools is critical for AI consultants. In this section, we explore popular programming languages like Python, R, and Julia, which are widely used in AI development. We provide hands-on examples of coding in Python, showcasing how to implement machine learning algorithms and data manipulation techniques. Additionally, readers will be introduced to AI libraries and frameworks, such as TensorFlow, PyTorch, and scikit-learn, which enable efficient AI model development and deployment.

2.3 Data Management and Preprocessing

The quality of data directly impacts the success of AI projects. In this section, we delve into data management and preprocessing techniques that AI consultants must master. Readers will learn how to handle data cleaning, missing value imputation, and feature scaling. Moreover, we discuss data exploration and visualization methods to gain deeper insights into datasets before model development. Understanding data preprocessing is crucial to ensure that AI models are trained on reliable and meaningful data.

Conclusion: Chapter 2 equips readers with a robust technical foundation, laying the groundwork for their journey to becoming proficient AI consultants. By understanding the mathematical principles behind AI algorithms, mastering programming languages and AI tools, and developing data management and preprocessing skills, readers are well-prepared to engage in practical AI projects. Armed with this technical prowess and a commitment to continuous learning, aspiring AI consultants are poised to thrive in the dynamic and innovative world of AI development.

2.1 Mathematics and Statistics for AI Consultants

Mathematics and statistics serve as the backbone of Artificial Intelligence (AI) algorithms and models. Aspiring AI consultants must develop a solid understanding of these foundational concepts to excel in the field. In this section, we explore the key mathematical and statistical principles that are essential for AI consultants.

a) **Linear Algebra:** Linear algebra is a fundamental branch of mathematics used extensively in AI. Matrices and vectors are central to representing data and mathematical operations in AI models. Concepts such as matrix multiplication, transpose, and inverse are essential for transformations and computations in AI algorithms. Linear algebra plays a crucial role in tasks like data preprocessing, feature engineering, and dimensionality reduction.

b) **Calculus:** Calculus is another essential branch of mathematics in AI development. It provides tools for optimizing AI models and understanding their behavior. Concepts like derivatives and gradients are crucial for training machine learning models through techniques like gradient descent. Optimization algorithms use calculus to find the minimum or maximum of functions, enabling AI models to converge to the best solutions

c) **Probability and Statistics:** Probability theory forms the basis of uncertainty modeling in AI. AI consultants use probability to estimate uncertainties in predictions, quantify risk, and assess the confidence of AI model outputs. Bayesian statistics plays a vital role in probabilistic AI models, Bayesian networks, and decision-making under uncertainty. Understanding statistical concepts like mean, variance, and hypothesis testing is essential for evaluating AI model performance and making data-driven decisions.

d) **Optimization:** Optimization is a core concept in AI, where the goal is to find the best parameters or settings for AI models. AI consultants use optimization techniques to fine-tune model parameters, minimizing errors and maximizing accuracy. Gradient-based optimization algorithms, such as stochastic gradient descent (SGD), are widely used in training neural networks and other machine learning models.

e) **Eigenvalues and Eigenvectors:** Eigenvalues and eigenvectors are important concepts in linear algebra used in dimensionality reduction techniques like Principal Component Analysis (PCA). AI consultants leverage these concepts to extract meaningful features from high-dimensional data, reducing computational complexity and improving model performance.

f) **Probability Distributions:** Understanding different probability distributions is crucial for modeling uncertainties in AI. Gaussian (normal) distributions are commonly used in AI models, but consultants must also be familiar with other distributions like binomial, Poisson, and exponential distributions. These distributions have applications in various AI tasks, such as generating synthetic data, simulating events, and uncertainty estimation.

g) **Random Variables and Monte Carlo Methods:** Random variables and Monte Carlo methods are integral to probabilistic AI models and simulations. AI consultants use Monte Carlo methods to approximate complex mathematical functions, perform Bayesian inference, and propagate uncertainties through AI models.

Conclusion: Mathematics and statistics are the building blocks of AI algorithms and models. AI consultants must develop a strong foundation in linear algebra, calculus, probability, and statistics to effectively design, develop, and optimize AI solutions. Understanding these mathematical and statistical principles empowers consultants to tackle complex AI challenges and make data-driven decisions, ultimately driving success in their AI consulting journey.

2.2 Programming Languages and Tools for AI Development

Programming languages and tools are the driving force behind AI development, enabling AI consultants to build sophisticated algorithms, design AI models, and analyze data efficiently. In this section, we explore the essential programming languages and AI tools that are fundamental for AI development and consulting.

a) **Python**: Python has emerged as the primary programming language for AI development due to its simplicity, readability, and versatility. Its extensive libraries, such as NumPy, pandas, and SciPy, provide powerful data manipulation and analysis capabilities. Python's user-friendly syntax makes it an ideal choice for AI consultants, allowing them to focus on AI concepts rather than complex coding structures.

b) **R:** R is a specialized programming language designed for statistical computing and data analysis. It is widely used in the AI and data science community, particularly for data exploration, visualization, and statistical modeling. R's vast collection of packages and libraries, like ggplot2 and caret, make it a valuable tool for AI consultants dealing with complex statistical analyses.

c) **Julia:** Julia is a high-level, high-performance programming language designed for scientific computing. It has gained popularity in AI research and development due to its speed and ability to seamlessly integrate with C and Fortran code. Julia's parallel computing capabilities make it well-suited for handling large datasets and performing computationally intensive tasks in AI applications.

d) **TensorFlow:** Developed by Google, TensorFlow is an open-source machine learning library known for its flexibility and scalability. It allows AI consultants to build and train various AI models, particularly deep learning models like neural networks. TensorFlow's ability to work efficiently with GPUs and TPUs (Tensor Processing Units) accelerates training and inference processes, making it a preferred choice for AI consultants dealing with large datasets.

e) **PyTorch:** PyTorch is another popular open-source deep learning library that provides dynamic computation graphs. Its user-friendly and intuitive interface makes it an attractive option for AI consultants experimenting with complex deep learning architectures. PyTorch's dynamic nature enables easy model debugging and development, making it a favorite among researchers and developers alike.

f) **Scikit-learn:** scikit-learn is a comprehensive machine learning library for Python, offering a wide range of algorithms for classification, regression, clustering, and more. AI consultants often use scikit-learn for quick prototyping and testing of machine learning models due to its simplicity and ease of integration with other Python libraries.

g) **Keras:** Keras is an open-source deep learning library built on top of TensorFlow and designed for fast and easy prototyping of neural networks. It provides a high-level API that simplifies the process of building and training deep learning models. AI consultants often use Keras for rapid experimentation and implementation of complex neural network architectures.

h) **Jupyter Notebooks:** Jupyter Notebooks are interactive computing environments that allow AI consultants to combine code, text, and visualizations in a single document. They are ideal for presenting AI analyses, sharing research findings, and collaborating with team members. Jupyter Notebooks promote reproducibility and facilitate clear documentation, making them valuable tools for AI development and consulting.

Conclusion:
Programming languages and AI tools are indispensable assets for AI consultants. Python, R, and Julia serve as versatile programming languages, with Python being the most widely used in AI development. TensorFlow and PyTorch are prominent deep learning libraries, while scikit-learn and Keras offer diverse machine learning capabilities. Jupyter Notebooks aid in code experimentation and documentation. Mastering these programming languages and AI tools empowers AI consultants to build, optimize, and deploy powerful AI models, delivering innovative solutions and insights to their clients with efficiency and precision.

2.3 Data Management and Preprocessing

Data management and preprocessing are critical steps in AI development and consulting. High-quality and well-prepared data are essential for building accurate and reliable AI models. In this section, we explore the key aspects of data management and preprocessing that AI consultants must master to ensure the success of their AI projects.

a) **Data Collection and Storage:** The first step in data management is data collection. AI consultants must identify relevant data sources and collect data that aligns with the project objectives. The data can come from various sources, including databases, APIs, sensors, web scraping, and more. Once collected, the data needs to be stored securely in a structured format to facilitate easy access and analysis.

b) **Data Cleaning:** Data is rarely perfect; it often contains errors, missing values, and inconsistencies. Data cleaning involves identifying and rectifying these issues to ensure data accuracy and reliability. AI consultants must employ techniques like imputation (filling in missing values), outlier removal, and data normalization to clean the data and make it suitable for analysis.

c) **Data Transformation:** Data transformation involves converting data into a format suitable for AI modeling. It may include scaling numerical features to a similar range, encoding categorical variables, and handling skewed distributions. Transformation ensures that all features are on the same scale and have a comparable impact on the AI model's performance.

d) **Feature Engineering:** Feature engineering is a critical step in data preprocessing where AI consultants create new features or modify existing ones to improve the AI model's performance. It involves selecting the most relevant features, creating interaction terms, and generating derived features to capture complex patterns in the data effectively.

e) **Data Splitting:** To evaluate the performance of an AI model, consultants need to divide the data into training, validation, and testing sets. Training data is used to train the model, validation data to fine-tune hyperparameters, and testing data to assess the model's generalization performance. Proper data splitting helps prevent overfitting and ensures that the AI model performs well on new, unseen data.

f) **Dealing with Imbalanced Data:** In many AI applications, the data may be imbalanced, meaning that one class or outcome is much more prevalent than others. AI consultants must address this issue to prevent biased models. Techniques like oversampling, undersampling, and generating synthetic data can help balance the data and improve model performance.

g) **Handling Text and Unstructured Data:** AI consultants often encounter text and unstructured data in their projects. Natural Language Processing (NLP) techniques, such as tokenization, stemming, and sentiment analysis, are employed to process and extract valuable insights from text data. Unstructured data, like images and audio, requires specialized preprocessing techniques to extract meaningful features for AI modeling.

h) **Data Visualization:** Data visualization is a powerful tool for understanding data patterns and trends. AI consultants use various visualization techniques, such as histograms, scatter plots, and heatmaps, to explore data and gain insights. Visualization aids in identifying potential issues, validating assumptions, and communicating findings to stakeholders effectively.

Conclusion:
Data management and preprocessing are fundamental steps in AI development that cannot be overlooked. AI consultants must collect relevant data, clean and preprocess it to ensure its quality, and transform it into a suitable format for AI modeling. Proper data splitting and handling of imbalanced data are crucial for developing robust and unbiased AI models. Skillful feature engineering and handling of text and unstructured data contribute to the success of AI projects. Data visualization aids in understanding data patterns and communicating results to stakeholders. By mastering these data management and preprocessing techniques, AI consultants can set a strong foundation for building accurate, reliable, and impactful AI solutions for their clients.

Chapter 3: Nurturing Your Problem-Solving Skills

In the dynamic field of AI consulting, strong problem-solving skills are essential for success. This chapter delves into the art of problem-solving and its significance in tackling complex AI challenges. As AI consultants, cultivating critical thinking and analytical abilities is crucial for approaching AI projects with creativity, efficiency, and effectiveness. Let's explore the first three topics covered in this chapter:

3.1 Critical Thinking and Analytical Abilities:

To excel in AI consulting, AI professionals must hone their critical thinking and analytical abilities. Critical thinking involves the ability to objectively analyze information, assess its validity, and draw well-reasoned conclusions. In AI projects, critical thinking allows consultants to identify underlying patterns, potential biases, and alternative solutions. Analytical abilities play a vital role in interpreting data, extracting meaningful insights, and making informed decisions throughout the consulting process.

3.2 Problem-Solving Frameworks for AI Projects:

As AI consultants tackle complex challenges, problem-solving frameworks serve as invaluable guides. These frameworks provide structured methodologies for approaching AI projects, ensuring a systematic and comprehensive analysis of the problem at hand. In this section, we introduce popular problem-solving frameworks such as DMAIC (Define, Measure, Analyze, Improve, Control), PDCA (Plan, Do, Check, Act), and Design Thinking. We explore how these frameworks can be tailored and applied to AI projects to facilitate creative ideation and effective solutions.

3.3 Understanding Business Challenges and Goals:

A fundamental aspect of successful AI consulting is understanding the business context and challenges faced by clients. AI consultants must actively engage with stakeholders to grasp their goals, pain points, and desired outcomes. By aligning AI initiatives with specific business objectives, consultants can create solutions that drive tangible value for clients. In this section, we explore effective techniques for conducting stakeholder interviews, analyzing business requirements, and translating them into actionable AI projects.

3.1 Critical Thinking and Analytical Abilities

Critical thinking and analytical abilities are fundamental skills for AI consultants, allowing them to approach complex problems with clarity and logic. These skills are at the core of successful AI development, as they enable consultants to analyze data, evaluate models, and make informed decisions. In this section, we delve deeper into the importance of critical thinking and analytical abilities in the context of AI consulting.

Data Analysis and Interpretation:

AI consultants deal with vast amounts of data, which require careful analysis and interpretation. Critical thinking allows consultants to identify patterns, trends, and insights from data, making sense of complex information. Analytical abilities help consultants apply statistical methods, data visualization, and machine learning techniques to extract meaningful conclusions from data sets, facilitating data-driven decision-making.

a) **Model Evaluation and Validation:** Evaluating AI models is a critical step in AI consulting. Consultants must critically analyze model performance metrics, such as accuracy, precision, recall, and F1 score, to assess the model's effectiveness. Analytical abilities aid in understanding model behavior, identifying potential biases, and validating model predictions against real-world outcomes. This process ensures that AI solutions are accurate, reliable, and trustworthy.

b) **Problem Reframing and Solution Exploration:** AI consultants often encounter ambiguous or ill-defined problems. Critical thinking enables them to reframe problems effectively, gaining a deeper understanding of the challenges at hand. Analytical abilities empower consultants to explore various solution approaches, considering the strengths and weaknesses of each option. By critically evaluating potential solutions, consultants can identify the most suitable path for addressing the problem.

c) **Debugging and Troubleshooting:** In AI development, consultants must debug and troubleshoot code and models regularly. Critical thinking guides them in systematically identifying errors and diagnosing issues in AI implementations. Analytical abilities help consultants narrow down potential causes of problems and devise effective solutions to fix them, streamlining the development process.

d) **Decision-Making and Risk Assessment:** AI consultants often face complex decisions with potential risks and uncertainties. Critical thinking allows consultants to weigh the pros and cons of different choices, considering the potential impact on the project and stakeholders. Analytical abilities support consultants in assessing risks and uncertainties associated with AI solutions, enabling them to make well-informed decisions and anticipate potential challenges.

e) **Adapting to New Challenges and Technologies:** The field of AI is continuously evolving, with new challenges and technologies emerging regularly. Critical thinking and analytical abilities empower consultants to adapt to these changes, quickly grasping new concepts and methodologies. Consultants can evaluate the suitability of emerging technologies for specific projects and incorporate them into their AI solutions.

f) **Continuous Learning and Improvement:** Critical thinking and analytical abilities drive a culture of continuous learning and improvement among AI consultants. By analyzing the outcomes of AI projects and reflecting on their methodologies, consultants identify opportunities for enhancement. This iterative learning process enhances their problem-solving skills and ensures that they stay at the forefront of AI advancements.

Conclusion: Critical thinking and analytical abilities are indispensable skills for AI consultants. These skills empower consultants to analyze data, evaluate AI models, and make well-informed decisions throughout the AI development process. By honing their critical thinking and analytical skills, AI consultants become adept problem solvers, capable of delivering innovative and effective AI solutions to their clients. Additionally, the ability to adapt to new challenges and technologies ensures that consultants remain valuable assets in the ever-evolving field of AI consulting.

3.2 Problem-Solving Frameworks for AI Projects

Problem-solving frameworks are systematic approaches that guide AI consultants through the complex process of developing AI solutions. These frameworks provide a structured and organized way to tackle AI projects, ensuring that consultants address challenges effectively and deliver valuable outcomes to their clients. In this section, we explore some popular problem-solving frameworks for AI projects.

CRISP-DM (Cross-Industry Standard Process for Data Mining):

CRISP-DM is one of the most widely used frameworks for data mining and AI projects. It consists of six key phases:

1. **Business Understanding:** Understand the business objectives, requirements, and constraints to frame the problem.

2. **Data Understanding:** Gather and assess data to identify relevant datasets for analysis.

3. **Data Preparation:** Clean, preprocess, and transform the data to make it suitable for AI modeling.

4. **Modeling:** Select and develop appropriate AI models to address the business problem.

5. Evaluation: Assess the performance of AI models and validate their results against objectives.

6. Deployment: Implement and deploy the AI solution into the operational environment.

CRISP-DM provides a clear roadmap for AI consultants, promoting a structured and iterative approach to AI development.

DMAIC (Define, Measure, Analyze, Improve, Control):

DMAIC is a problem-solving framework used in process improvement and optimization, which can be adapted to AI projects. It involves the following steps:

1. Define: Clearly define the problem, project goals, and key performance indicators (KPIs).

2. Measure: Collect and analyze data to measure the current state and establish baseline performance.

3. Analyze: Identify root causes, patterns, and opportunities for improvement based on data analysis.

4. Improve: Develop and implement AI solutions to address the identified issues and achieve project goals.

5. Control: Implement measures to monitor and sustain the improvements over time.

DMAIC helps AI consultants focus on data-driven decision-making and continuous improvement throughout the AI project lifecycle.

OODA (Observe, Orient, Decide, Act):

The OODA loop is a decision-making and problem-solving framework that originated in military strategy but can be applied to AI projects. It involves the following steps:

1. Observe: Gather data, monitor AI model performance, and assess the current state of the project.

2. Orient: Analyze the data, interpret results, and understand the implications for decision-making

3. Decide: Based on the analysis, make informed decisions and choose the appropriate course of action.

4. Act: Implement the decisions and deploy AI solutions, continuously monitoring their performance.

The OODA loop emphasizes adaptability and agility, enabling AI consultants to respond quickly to changing circumstances in AI projects.

Design Thinking:

Design thinking is a human-centered problem-solving approach that fosters empathy, creativity, and innovation. It involves five stages:

1. **Empathize:** Understand the needs and pain points of end-users and stakeholders.
2. **Define:** Frame the problem statement based on user insights and requirements.
3. **Ideate:** Generate a wide range of creative ideas and potential AI solutions.
4. **Prototype:** Develop prototypes or mock-ups to test and validate AI concepts.
5. **Test:** Gather feedback from users and stakeholders, refining and iterating the AI solutions.

Design thinking encourages AI consultants to approach problems from the perspective of end-users, ensuring that AI solutions are user-friendly and aligned with their needs.

Conclusion: Problem-solving frameworks are invaluable tools for AI consultants, providing systematic approaches to tackle complex AI projects effectively. CRISP-DM, DMAIC, OODA, and design thinking are among the popular problem-solving frameworks that guide consultants through different aspects of AI development. By leveraging these frameworks, AI consultants can structure their projects, make data-driven decisions, and deliver impactful AI solutions that meet business objectives and exceed client expectations.

3.3 Understanding Business Challenges and Goals

In AI consulting, a deep understanding of the client's business challenges and goals is a fundamental starting point for success. AI consultants must align their efforts with the client's vision, mission, and objectives to deliver AI solutions that generate tangible value. In this section, we explore the importance of understanding business challenges and goals in AI consulting and how consultants can gain the necessary insights.

a) **Client Engagement and Communication:** Effective communication with clients is the key to understanding their business challenges and goals. AI consultants must engage in active listening and open dialogue to comprehend the client's pain points, aspirations, and specific requirements. Regular meetings, workshops, and interviews with key stakeholders enable consultants to gather crucial insights about the business context and expectations.

b) **Domain Expertise:** To understand business challenges and goals, AI consultants need domain expertise in the client's industry or sector. Familiarity with the client's market dynamics, competitive landscape, and regulatory environment helps consultants grasp the unique challenges faced by the client and design tailored AI solutions that align with industry-specific needs.

c) **Problem Framing and Scoping:** AI consultants must collaboratively frame the business problem with the client, ensuring that it is well-defined and aligns with the overarching business goals. Clear problem scoping helps consultants focus their efforts on the most critical aspects of the project, preventing scope creep and optimizing resource allocation.

d) **Business Process Analysis:** Conducting a thorough analysis of the client's business processes is essential to understanding where AI solutions can add the most value. AI consultants must identify pain points, inefficiencies, and bottlenecks in the existing processes. This analysis provides insights into areas where AI automation, optimization, or decision support can drive significant improvements.

e) **Quantifiable Objectives:** AI solutions should be designed with quantifiable objectives and key performance indicators (KPIs) that align with the client's business goals. Clear and measurable objectives enable both the client and the consultant to assess the success and impact of the AI project accurately.

f) **Risk Assessment:** Understanding the potential risks and challenges associated with AI implementations is crucial for effective problem-solving. AI consultants must conduct risk assessments, considering factors like data quality, privacy concerns, regulatory compliance, and potential ethical implications. Mitigating these risks ensures the responsible and sustainable deployment of AI solutions.

g) **Scalability and Long-Term Impact:** AI consultants should consider the scalability and long-term impact of their solutions. Scalable AI solutions can adapt to changing business needs and accommodate increased data volumes and user demands. Additionally, understanding the long-term impact helps consultants design AI solutions that align with the client's strategic vision and growth trajectory.

h) **Value Proposition and Return on Investment (ROI):** Ultimately, AI consulting revolves around delivering value to the client. Consultants must articulate a clear value proposition and demonstrate the expected ROI of their AI solutions. Understanding the client's budget constraints and cost-benefit considerations helps consultants propose AI projects that offer compelling returns.

Conclusion:
Understanding business challenges and goals is the foundation of successful AI consulting. AI consultants must actively engage with clients, gain domain expertise, and analyze business processes to frame well-defined problems

and objectives. Quantifiable objectives, risk assessments, and considerations of scalability and long-term impact ensure that AI solutions deliver sustained value to the client. By comprehending the client's vision and aligning AI solutions with their business goals, AI consultants become strategic partners in driving innovation, efficiency, and growth for their clients.

Part 2: AI Consulting Process

In Part 2, we delve into the AI consulting process, which encompasses the systematic steps and methodologies AI consultants follow to design, develop, and deploy AI solutions. The AI consulting process enables consultants to address complex business challenges effectively and deliver AI-driven insights and innovations to their clients. This part covers the key stages of the AI consulting process:

Stage 1: Project Scoping and Understanding Client Needs

In this initial stage, AI consultants engage with the client to understand their specific business challenges, objectives, and requirements. The consultants collaboratively define the scope of the AI project, identifying the key deliverables, timelines, and resources needed. Active communication and domain expertise are essential during this stage to gain a deep understanding of the client's needs and context.

Stage 2: Data Gathering and Preprocessing

Data forms the foundation of AI solutions. In this stage, AI consultants gather and analyze relevant data from various sources. They perform data preprocessing, which includes data cleaning, transformation, and feature engineering, to ensure data quality and suitability for AI modeling. Proper data management and preprocessing are critical to building accurate and robust AI models.

Stage 3: AI Model Development

AI consultants select appropriate AI algorithms and models based on the project requirements and data characteristics. They train and validate the AI models using the prepared data. This stage involves iteratively fine-tuning the model parameters and hyperparameters to optimize performance. Consultants leverage their analytical abilities to evaluate different models and choose the most suitable one for the project.

Stage 4: Model Evaluation and Testing

The AI models undergo rigorous evaluation and testing to assess their performance and generalization capabilities. Consultants use various metrics and testing methodologies to ensure that the AI models meet the defined objectives and KPIs. Model validation against real-world data is essential to validate the reliability of AI predictions and recommendations.

Stage 5: AI Solution Deployment

Once the AI models are validated, AI consultants proceed to deploy the solutions into the client's operational environment. This stage involves integrating the AI solutions with existing systems, setting up monitoring mechanisms, and ensuring seamless functionality. Consultants must also provide necessary training and support to the client's team to ensure effective adoption and utilization of the AI solutions.

Stage 6: Post-Deployment Monitoring and Maintenance

AI solutions require continuous monitoring to ensure their ongoing performance and effectiveness. Consultants must establish mechanisms for monitoring and collecting feedback from users to identify potential issues and areas for improvement. Regular maintenance and updates are essential to keep the AI solutions up-to-date and aligned with the client's evolving needs.

Stage 7: Insights Delivery and Client Support

AI consulting goes beyond model development; it involves providing actionable insights and guidance to clients. AI consultants must communicate the results of their analysis effectively, offering clear explanations and actionable recommendations. Client support and collaboration are crucial to building long-term partnerships and ensuring the successful implementation of AI solutions.

Stage 8: Continuous Improvement and Innovation

The AI consulting process is not linear; it involves continuous improvement and innovation. Consultants must reflect on the outcomes of their AI projects, learn from successes and challenges, and apply these insights to future projects. A culture of continuous learning and innovation drives the growth and success of AI consulting endeavors.

Conclusion: Part 2 of the book covers the AI consulting process, which consists of systematic stages from understanding client needs to delivering AI solutions and supporting their deployment. Through effective communication, data gathering, and model development, AI consultants address business challenges and generate valuable insights. Continuous monitoring, client support, and a commitment to innovation ensure that AI solutions deliver ongoing value to clients and position AI consultants as strategic partners in driving business transformation through artificial intelligence.

Chapter 4: Scoping AI Projects

In the realm of AI consulting, the successful execution of projects hinges on meticulous planning and scoping. This chapter delves into the critical process of defining project objectives and scope, assessing feasibility and resources, and devising risk assessment and mitigation strategies. By mastering these essential elements, AI consultants can lay the groundwork for successful project execution and deliver AI solutions that drive tangible results. Let's explore the first three topics covered in this chapter:

4.1 Defining Project Objectives and Scope:

Clear and well-defined project objectives are the foundation of any successful AI consulting engagement. This section delves into the art of collaborating with clients to identify specific goals, KPIs, and deliverables. By establishing a shared understanding of project scope, consultants can avoid potential misunderstandings and ensure alignment with client expectations. We explore techniques for crafting comprehensive project charters and setting achievable milestones to guide the project's trajectory.

4.2 Assessing Feasibility and Resources:

Before diving into an AI project, AI consultants must conduct a rigorous feasibility assessment. This involves evaluating the technical and organizational capabilities required for successful project execution. Consultants must identify the availability and accessibility of relevant data, the computational resources needed for model development, and the expertise required to handle specific AI technologies. By conducting a thorough feasibility analysis, consultants can proactively address potential challenges and design appropriate strategies to overcome them.

4.3 Risk Assessment and Mitigation Strategies:

In the dynamic landscape of AI projects, uncertainties and risks are inevitable. This section explores various risk assessment techniques to identify potential threats that could impact project timelines, budgets, or overall success. Consultants will learn to anticipate and categorize risks related to data quality, model performance, regulatory compliance, and more. Moreover, we delve into the formulation of robust mitigation strategies that enable proactive risk management and contingency planning.

Conclusion: Throughout this chapter, we emphasize the iterative nature of scoping AI projects. AI consultants must be flexible and adaptive, recognizing that project objectives, feasibility, and risks may evolve as they progress through the consulting journey. By diligently scoping AI projects and devising comprehensive strategies, AI consultants can optimize project outcomes and deliver AI solutions that drive transformative value for their clients.

4.1 Defining Project Objectives and Scope

Defining clear project objectives and scope is a crucial step in AI consulting. It lays the foundation for a successful AI project by providing a clear roadmap and alignment between the AI consultant and the client's expectations. In this section, we explore the process of defining project objectives and scope and its importance in AI consulting.

a) **Understanding Client Needs:** The first step in defining project objectives and scope is to thoroughly understand the client's needs and requirements. AI consultants engage in active communication with the client to gain insights into their business challenges, goals, and desired outcomes. This understanding forms the basis for establishing the project's purpose and objectives.

b) **Identifying Key Deliverables:** AI consultants work closely with the client to identify the key deliverables expected from the AI project. These deliverables could be AI models, data analysis reports, interactive dashboards, or other actionable insights. Clearly identifying the deliverables helps set client expectations and ensures that the project outcomes align with the client's needs.

c) **Establishing Measurable Goals:** Project objectives should be specific, measurable, achievable, relevant, and time-bound (SMART). By establishing measurable goals, AI consultants and clients can objectively assess the success of the project. This helps in evaluating the project's impact on the client's business and justifying the return on investment (ROI) of the AI project.

d) **Defining Project Scope:** Project scope defines the boundaries and limitations of the AI project. It outlines what will be included in the project and, equally importantly, what will be excluded. The scope helps prevent scope creep and ensures that the project remains focused and achievable. It includes details about the AI models to be developed, data sources to be used, and the industries or business areas to be covered.

e) **Assessing Technical Feasibility:** AI consultants assess the technical feasibility of the project based on the available data, AI algorithms, and computational resources. This evaluation helps in identifying any technical challenges or limitations that may impact the project's success. If certain aspects of the project are not technically feasible, consultants can work with the client to find alternative solutions or adjust the project scope accordingly.

f) **Considering Resource Constraints:** AI projects require various resources, including human expertise, computing power, and financial investments. Consultants consider the available resources and constraints during the project scoping process. This ensures that the project is realistically planned and feasible within the client's budget and timeline.

g) **Collaborating with Stakeholders:** Defining project objectives and scope is a collaborative effort involving key stakeholders, including the client's management team and end-users. AI consultants actively engage with stakeholders to gather feedback, gain insights, and incorporate their perspectives into the project scope. This collaborative approach fosters a sense of ownership and ensures that the project meets the needs of all stakeholders.

h) **Documenting the Project Scope:** Once the project objectives and scope are defined, AI consultants document them in a clear and comprehensive manner. This project scope document serves as a reference guide throughout the AI project, helping to align all team members and stakeholders towards a common vision.

Conclusion: Defining project objectives and scope is a critical step in AI consulting. It ensures that AI consultants and clients are aligned on project goals, deliverables, and constraints. A well-defined scope provides a clear direction for the AI project, enabling efficient resource allocation, effective project management, and successful project outcomes. By collaboratively establishing measurable objectives and setting realistic project scope, AI consultants deliver valuable AI solutions that meet client expectations and drive meaningful impact in their business.

4.2 Assessing Feasibility and Resources

In AI consulting, assessing the feasibility of a project and evaluating the available resources are crucial steps that determine the success and viability of the AI endeavor. These assessments help AI consultants and clients understand the project's technical and practical limitations, ensuring that the project can be executed efficiently and effectively. In this section, we explore the process of assessing feasibility and resources in AI consulting.

Technical Feasibility:

AI consultants evaluate the technical feasibility of a project by considering the following factors:

a) **Data Availability and Quality:** AI projects heavily rely on data. Consultants assess the availability and quality of data needed for the project. They examine whether the data required for AI model training is accessible, sufficient, and representative of the problem at hand. Inadequate or poor-quality data can hinder the development and performance of AI models.

b) **AI Algorithms and Models:** Consultants analyze the suitability of AI algorithms and models for the specific problem. They consider factors like the complexity of the problem, available data, and the required level of interpretability. Choosing the right algorithms and models is critical for achieving accurate and reliable AI solutions.

c) **Computational Resources:** AI projects often require substantial computational resources, especially for training complex deep learning models. Consultants assess the availability of computing power, including GPUs and TPUs, to handle the computational demands of the project.

d) **Integration with Existing Systems:** For AI solutions to be effective, they must seamlessly integrate with the client's existing systems and workflows. Consultants evaluate the feasibility of integrating AI solutions into the client's infrastructure and identify any potential technical challenges.

Resource Assessment:

AI consultants conduct a thorough assessment of the resources required for the project. This includes:

a) **Human Resources:** Consultants consider the expertise and skill sets required to execute the project. They assess the availability of data scientists, AI engineers, domain experts, and other team members needed to work on the project.

b) **Financial Resources:** AI projects may involve costs related to data acquisition, computing infrastructure, software licenses, and human resources. Consultants work with the client to determine the budget and funding available for the project.

c) **Timeframe:** Consultants evaluate the project timeline and deadlines to ensure that the project can be completed within the required timeframe. They consider any time constraints imposed by the client's business needs.

d) **External Support:** In some cases, consultants may require external support, such as collaboration with research institutions, access to specialized AI tools, or partnerships with data providers. Assessing external support helps in planning for collaborative efforts.

e) **Risk Assessment:** As part of feasibility assessment, AI consultants conduct risk analysis to identify potential obstacles and challenges. This includes evaluating risks related to data privacy, regulatory compliance, model interpretability, and ethical considerations. Consultants develop risk mitigation strategies to address these challenges and ensure responsible AI implementation.

f) **Communication with Stakeholders:** Feasibility and resource assessments are collaborative efforts involving key stakeholders, including the client's management team and end-users. Consultants actively engage with stakeholders to gather input, set expectations, and address any concerns related to the project's feasibility and resource requirements.

Conclusion: Assessing feasibility and resources is a critical stage in AI consulting that enables consultants and clients to make informed decisions about the project's viability and success. By evaluating technical feasibility, resource availability, and potential risks, AI consultants can plan and execute projects effectively, delivering valuable AI solutions that align with client objectives and contribute to business transformation. Effective communication and collaboration with stakeholders ensure that the project scope is realistic, achievable, and positioned for success.

4.3 Risk Assessment and Mitigation Strategies

In AI consulting, risk assessment is an essential process that identifies potential challenges, uncertainties, and vulnerabilities in the AI project. By proactively evaluating risks, AI consultants can develop mitigation strategies to address these issues and ensure the responsible and successful implementation of AI solutions. In this section, we explore the importance of risk assessment and various mitigation strategies employed in AI consulting.

a) **Data Quality and Privacy Risks:** Data forms the backbone of AI solutions, and data quality and privacy risks are critical concerns. AI consultants assess the quality and integrity of data sources, identifying potential issues such as missing values, outliers, and biases. Data privacy risks involve the protection of sensitive information and compliance with data regulations. To mitigate these risks, consultants implement data anonymization, encryption, and access controls, ensuring data security and privacy.

b) **Bias and Fairness Risks:** AI models can inherit biases present in the data used for training, leading to unfair or discriminatory outcomes. AI consultants must analyze the data and model results for potential bias and assess the fairness of the AI solution across different demographic groups. Mitigation strategies include using diverse and representative datasets, adopting debiasing techniques, and implementing fairness-aware learning algorithms.

c) **Interpretability and Explainability Risks:** Complex AI models, such as deep learning networks, are often considered black boxes, making it challenging to interpret their decision-making processes. Lack of model interpretability can lead to distrust and hinder adoption. To mitigate this risk, consultants can employ explainable AI techniques, such as LIME or SHAP, to provide insights into model decisions and enhance transparency.

d) **Overfitting and Generalization Risks:** Overfitting occurs when an AI model performs well on the training data but poorly on new, unseen data. To mitigate overfitting risks, consultants use techniques like cross-validation, regularization, and early stopping during model training. Ensuring proper data splitting and validation also helps assess the model's generalization capabilities.

e) **Technical and Resource Risks:** AI projects may encounter technical challenges related to algorithm implementation, scalability, and computational resources. Consultants assess the availability and adequacy of computational infrastructure to handle the project's requirements. Mitigation strategies include choosing scalable algorithms, optimizing code, and allocating sufficient computing power for model training and deployment.

f) **Ethical and Societal Risks:** AI solutions can have far-reaching societal impacts, and ethical considerations are crucial in AI consulting. Consultants must be aware of potential negative consequences, such as job displacement or privacy breaches. To mitigate ethical risks, consultants follow ethical guidelines, involve ethics experts in project planning, and conduct regular ethical reviews of AI solutions.

g) **Integration and Change Management Risks:** Deploying AI solutions into existing business processes may face integration challenges. Consultants assess the readiness of the client's systems for AI implementation and evaluate potential disruptions to the workflow. Mitigation strategies include conducting pilot tests, providing training to end-users, and ensuring a smooth transition to the new AI system.

h) **Data Security and Cybersecurity Risks:** AI solutions may be susceptible to cyberattacks and data breaches. Consultants implement robust security measures, including encryption, access controls, and regular system audits. Security testing and continuous monitoring are crucial for detecting and mitigating cybersecurity risks.

Conclusion:
Risk assessment and mitigation strategies are vital components of AI consulting that ensure the responsible and successful deployment of AI solutions. By proactively identifying potential risks and developing mitigation plans, AI consultants can address challenges and uncertainties that may arise during the project. Ethical considerations, data privacy, and model interpretability are key focus areas in risk mitigation. Effective risk management empowers consultants to deliver AI solutions that generate value, align with client objectives, and have a positive impact on businesses and society.

Chapter 5: Data Collection and Preparation

In the world of AI consulting, data forms the bedrock upon which AI models are built. Chapter 5 delves into the crucial aspects of data sourcing, collection, cleaning, and ensuring privacy and security. As AI consultants, mastering these data-related considerations is vital for creating accurate, reliable, and ethically sound AI solutions. Let's explore the first three topics covered in this chapter:

5.1 Data Sourcing and Collection Techniques:

The process of sourcing and collecting data is a critical step in AI projects. This section guides AI consultants through effective data acquisition strategies, considering both public and private data sources. We explore various data collection techniques, such as web scraping, APIs, surveys, and data partnerships. Additionally, we address the importance of adhering to legal and ethical guidelines for data acquisition and ensuring that the collected data aligns with the project's objectives.

5.2 Data Cleaning and Preprocessing:

Real-world data is rarely perfect, and this imperfection can significantly impact AI model performance. AI consultants must become proficient in data cleaning and preprocessing techniques to handle missing values, outliers, and inconsistencies. This section provides hands-on methods for data cleaning, normalization, feature scaling, and handling imbalanced datasets. We also discuss the implications of data preprocessing choices on model outcomes and how to strike the right balance.

5.3 Dealing with Data Privacy and Security:

As AI consultants handle sensitive and personal data, ensuring data privacy and security is paramount. This section delves into the ethical and legal obligations of safeguarding data privacy, especially when dealing with personal information. We explore techniques for data anonymization, encryption, and secure storage to protect data from unauthorized access. Additionally, we address the importance of transparency with clients and stakeholders about data handling practices to build trust and maintain compliance.

Conclusion: By mastering the art of data sourcing, cleaning, and privacy, AI consultants can build robust AI models that are not only technically sound but also ethically responsible. Throughout this chapter, we emphasize the need for continuous monitoring and adherence to data best practices to ensure data quality and maintain the highest standards of data privacy and security in AI consulting projects.

5.1 Data Sourcing and Collection Techniques

Data sourcing and collection are critical steps in AI consulting, as they lay the groundwork for building effective AI models. The success of an AI project heavily relies on the availability of high-quality and relevant data. In this section, we explore various data sourcing and collection techniques used by AI consultants to acquire the data needed for AI model development.

a) **Internal Data Sources:** AI consultants start by exploring the client's internal data sources, which may include databases, customer records, transaction logs, and operational data. Internal data is often rich in domain-specific information and offers insights into the client's unique business processes.

b) **External Data Sources:** AI consultants may also leverage external data sources to supplement the client's internal data. These sources can include publicly available datasets, open data repositories, government databases, and industry-specific data providers. External data can enrich the AI models and provide additional context for analysis.

c) **Web Scraping:** Web scraping is a technique used to extract data from websites and online sources. AI consultants can use web scraping to gather data from relevant websites, forums, social media platforms, and news articles. This data can provide valuable insights for sentiment analysis, trend monitoring, and market research.

d) **Surveys and Questionnaires:** Surveys and questionnaires are valuable data collection techniques for gathering specific information from target audiences. AI consultants design and distribute surveys to clients' customers, employees, or stakeholders to collect structured data for AI analysis.

e) **IoT Devices and Sensors:** In industries with IoT (Internet of Things) implementations, AI consultants can collect data from various IoT devices and sensors. IoT-generated data provides real-time insights and enables predictive maintenance, process optimization, and other AI applications.

f) **Audio and Video Data:** AI consultants may work with audio and video data in projects that involve speech recognition, natural language processing, or computer vision. Techniques like audio transcription and video frame analysis are used to convert unstructured data into usable formats.

g) **Historical Data Repositories:** Historical data repositories within organizations often contain valuable information collected over time. AI consultants can analyze this historical data to identify trends, patterns, and historical performance, enabling predictive modeling and decision support.

h) **Mobile Apps and User Interactions:** In projects that involve user behavior analysis or personalized recommendations, AI consultants can collect data from mobile apps and online platforms. User interactions, clicks, and preferences are valuable for understanding user behavior and preferences.

i) **Data Partnerships:** In some cases, AI consultants establish partnerships with third-party data providers or research institutions to access specialized data. Data partnerships can enrich the AI project with diverse and valuable datasets.

Conclusion: Data sourcing and collection techniques are vital for AI consulting projects. AI consultants use a combination of internal and external data sources, web scraping, surveys, IoT devices, and specialized partnerships to acquire relevant and high-quality data. Careful data sourcing and collection ensure that the data used for AI model development is representative, unbiased, and aligned with the project's objectives. By employing appropriate data collection techniques, AI consultants set the stage for effective AI analysis, decision-making, and the creation of valuable AI solutions for their clients.

5.2 Data Cleaning and Preprocessing

Data cleaning and preprocessing are essential steps in AI consulting that involve transforming raw data into a clean, structured, and usable format. High-quality data is fundamental to building accurate and robust AI models, as the performance of AI algorithms heavily depends on the data used for training and testing. In this section, we explore the significance of data cleaning and preprocessing in AI consulting and the key techniques employed.

Data Cleaning:

Data cleaning is the process of identifying and rectifying errors, inconsistencies, and inaccuracies in the data. Common data cleaning tasks include:

a) **Handling Missing Values:** AI consultants identify and deal with missing data points, either by imputing values based on statistical methods or by removing the corresponding data instances if appropriate.

b) **Removing Duplicates:** Duplicate records can lead to bias and distort the analysis. AI consultants eliminate duplicate data points to ensure data integrity.

c) **Standardizing Data:** Standardizing data units and formats ensures uniformity and consistency across the dataset, making it easier to analyze and interpret.

Data Preprocessing:

Data preprocessing involves transforming raw data into a format suitable for AI modeling. Key data preprocessing techniques include:

a) **Feature Scaling:** Scaling features to a similar range prevents some features from dominating others during model training. Common scaling methods include normalization and standardization.

b) **Feature Encoding:** Categorical variables are encoded into numerical format so that they can be used in AI models. Techniques like one-hot encoding and label encoding are used for this purpose.

c) **Handling Outliers:** Outliers are extreme values that can skew the analysis. AI consultants can choose to remove outliers or transform them to make the data more representative.

d) **Feature Engineering:** Feature engineering involves creating new features or transforming existing features to improve model performance. Domain knowledge plays a crucial role in identifying relevant features for AI modeling.

Data Validation and Integrity Checks:

AI consultants perform data validation to ensure the accuracy and reliability of the data. This includes cross-checking data against known reference values, performing data consistency checks, and validating the data against business rules.

a) **Dealing with Imbalanced Data:** In many real-world scenarios, data can be imbalanced, where one class or outcome is significantly more prevalent than others. AI consultants use techniques such as oversampling, undersampling, or using specialized algorithms like SMOTE to address class imbalance and prevent biased model training.

b) **Data Reduction Techniques:** For large datasets with high dimensionality, data reduction techniques like principal component analysis (PCA) or feature selection are employed to reduce the number of features while preserving the most important information.

c) **Data Visualization:** Data visualization is an integral part of data preprocessing, allowing AI consultants to gain insights into the data distribution, identify patterns, and visually verify data integrity.

Conclusion: Data cleaning and preprocessing are essential steps in AI consulting that ensure data quality and prepare the data for effective AI modeling. By cleaning data to remove errors and inconsistencies and preprocessing data to make it suitable for AI algorithms, consultants lay the foundation for building accurate and reliable AI models. Proper data cleaning and preprocessing contribute to the success of AI projects, enabling consultants to deliver valuable insights and solutions that meet client objectives and drive business transformation.

5.3 Dealing with Data Privacy and Security

Data privacy and security are paramount considerations in AI consulting. As AI projects involve handling vast amounts of data, protecting sensitive information is crucial to maintain trust with clients and comply with data regulations. In this section, we explore the importance of data privacy and security in AI consulting and the key measures employed to safeguard data.

a) **Data Privacy Regulations:** AI consultants must be well-versed in data privacy regulations that apply to the client's region and industry. Regulations like the General Data Protection Regulation (GDPR) in Europe or the California Consumer Privacy Act (CCPA) in the United States impose strict requirements on how personal data should be collected, processed, and stored.

b) **Anonymization and Pseudonymization:** To protect personal data, AI consultants use techniques like data anonymization and pseudonymization. Anonymization involves removing or encrypting any personally identifiable information from the dataset, making it impossible to identify individuals. Pseudonymization replaces identifiable information with pseudonyms, ensuring that only authorized parties can link the data to specific individuals.

c) **Access Controls and Data Governance:** AI consultants implement access controls and data governance practices to limit access to sensitive data. This ensures that only authorized personnel can access and process the data. Role-based access control (RBAC) and data access logs are common measures to enforce data security.

d) **Secure Data Transmission:** During data collection and sharing, AI consultants use secure communication protocols like HTTPS and encryption to protect data from unauthorized interception or tampering.

e) **Secure Data Storage:** Data storage systems must be designed with robust security measures to protect data at rest. Consultants use encryption techniques to ensure that even if data is accessed illegally, it remains unintelligible without the appropriate decryption keys.

f) **Regular Data Audits:** AI consultants conduct regular data audits to assess data privacy and security compliance. Audits identify vulnerabilities, assess data handling practices, and verify adherence to data privacy regulations.

g) **Data Retention Policies:** AI consultants work with clients to establish data retention policies that determine how long data should be retained. Retaining data for longer than necessary increases security risks and exposes data to potential breaches.

h) **Secure Model Deployment:** When deploying AI models, consultants ensure that data privacy measures are maintained. For instance, AI models designed for edge computing or distributed deployment must incorporate privacy-preserving techniques to protect sensitive data at the source.

i) **Ethical Considerations**: AI consultants address ethical considerations, such as ensuring fairness and transparency in AI decision-making. Ethical AI practices promote responsible AI deployment that respects user rights and prevents discriminatory outcomes.

Conclusion: Data privacy and security are fundamental principles in AI consulting. By implementing data anonymization, pseudonymization, access controls, and secure data transmission and storage, AI consultants protect sensitive information from unauthorized access and breaches. Adhering to data privacy regulations and conducting regular data audits ensures compliance and reinforces client trust. Ethical considerations in AI decision-making promote responsible AI implementations that respect user rights and societal values. By prioritizing data privacy and security, AI consultants foster a culture of data responsibility and deliver AI solutions that prioritize client confidentiality and build long-term client partnerships.

Chapter 6: AI Model Selection and Development

In the world of AI consulting, selecting the right AI model and implementing it effectively are crucial steps in building successful AI solutions. Chapter 6 explores the diverse landscape of AI models, including machine learning, deep learning, natural language processing (NLP), and more. AI consultants must be well-versed in the strengths and limitations of these models to make informed decisions about their suitability for specific tasks. Let's explore the first three topics covered in this chapter:

6.1 Understanding Various AI Models (Machine Learning, Deep Learning, NLP, etc.):

AI encompasses a rich spectrum of models and techniques, each tailored to different problem domains. In this section, we provide an overview of various AI models, including traditional machine learning algorithms like linear regression, decision trees, and support vector machines. We then delve into the fascinating world of deep learning, with neural networks, convolutional neural networks (CNNs), and recurrent neural networks (RNNs) taking center stage. Additionally, we explore the transformative impact of natural language processing (NLP) models in understanding and generating human language.

6.2 Evaluating Model Suitability for Specific Tasks:

Selecting the most suitable AI model for a given task is a critical decision in AI consulting. This section equips AI consultants with techniques to evaluate model performance, complexity, and resource requirements for specific tasks. We discuss the importance of matching AI models with the characteristics of the dataset and the desired output. Consultants will learn to assess model interpretability, explainability, and scalability, aligning the selected model with the overall project goals.

6.3 Implementing and Fine-Tuning AI Models:

Building AI models is an iterative and resource-intensive process. In this section, we guide AI consultants through the practical steps of implementing AI models in various frameworks, such as TensorFlow or PyTorch. We explore best practices for model initialization, training, and optimization. Fine-tuning AI models for enhanced performance is an essential skill that AI consultants will learn to refine through hyperparameter tuning and regularization techniques.

Conclusion: By developing a profound understanding of AI models and their capabilities, AI consultants can make informed decisions, confidently choose the right model for specific tasks, and optimize the implementation to deliver high-quality AI solutions. The chapter emphasizes the significance of staying updated with the latest advancements in AI models and techniques to stay at the cutting edge of AI consulting. As we embark on the journey of exploring AI models and their applications, AI consultants will gain the expertise needed to create transformative AI solutions that elevate business outcomes for their clients.

6.1 Understanding Various AI Models (Machine Learning, Deep Learning, NLP, etc.)

In AI consulting, understanding various AI models is essential for selecting the right approach to solve specific problems. AI encompasses a wide range of techniques, each with its strengths and limitations. In this section, we explore the main categories of AI models, including Machine Learning, Deep Learning, Natural Language Processing (NLP), and more.

Machine Learning:

Machine Learning (ML) is a subset of AI that focuses on algorithms and statistical techniques that enable computers to learn from data and make predictions or decisions without being explicitly programmed. There are three primary types of ML:

a) **Supervised Learning:** In supervised learning, the model is trained on labeled data, where the input features and corresponding output labels are known. The model learns to map inputs to outputs, enabling it to make predictions on new, unseen data.

b) **Unsupervised Learning:** In unsupervised learning, the model is trained on unlabeled data. The objective is to discover patterns, structures, or relationships in the data without explicit guidance. Clustering and dimensionality reduction are common unsupervised learning tasks.

c) **Reinforcement Learning:** Reinforcement learning involves an agent learning to make decisions by interacting with an environment. The agent receives feedback in the form of rewards or penalties, guiding it towards achieving specific goals.

Deep Learning:

Deep Learning (DL) is a subset of Machine Learning that utilizes artificial neural networks inspired by the structure of the human brain. Deep Learning models are capable of automatically learning hierarchical representations from data. Key concepts in DL include:

a) **Neural Networks:** Neural networks consist of layers of interconnected nodes (neurons). Each layer processes and transforms the data, leading to progressively abstract representations.

b) **Convolutional Neural Networks (CNNs):** CNNs are specialized neural networks for image and video analysis. They use convolutional layers to detect patterns and features in images.

c) **Recurrent Neural Networks (RNNs):** RNNs are designed to process sequential data, such as time series or natural language. They have loops that allow information to persist across time steps.

d) **Transformer-based Models:** Transformers are a type of deep learning architecture known for their success in natural language processing tasks. They use self-attention mechanisms to process sequential data.

Natural Language Processing (NLP):

NLP focuses on enabling computers to understand, interpret, and generate human language. NLP models have revolutionized language-related tasks, including:

a) **Text Classification:** Assigning text into predefined categories or classes, such as sentiment analysis or topic classification.

b) **Named Entity Recognition (NER):** Identifying entities like names of people, places, or organizations within text.

c) **Machine Translation:** Translating text from one language to another.

d) **Text Generation:** Generating human-like text, such as chatbots or language models.

Computer Vision:

Computer Vision involves teaching computers to interpret visual information from images and videos. Common tasks in computer vision include:

a) **Object Detection:** Identifying and locating specific objects within an image.

b) **Image Segmentation:** Dividing an image into segments and assigning labels to each segment.

c) **Image Captioning:** Generating natural language descriptions for images.

Reinforcement Learning:

Reinforcement Learning (RL) focuses on training agents to make decisions in an environment to maximize cumulative rewards. RL is commonly used in robotics, game playing, and autonomous systems.

Conclusion: Understanding various AI models is crucial in AI consulting. Each category of models offers unique capabilities and is suited for specific tasks. Machine Learning provides supervised, unsupervised, and reinforcement learning approaches, while Deep Learning excels in complex data representations. NLP enables language understanding, and computer vision addresses image and video analysis. By comprehending the strengths and applications of different AI models, consultants can select the most appropriate approach to deliver effective AI solutions that align with client objectives and drive business value.

6.1 Evaluating Model Suitability for Specific Tasks

In AI consulting, evaluating model suitability is a crucial step to ensure that the chosen AI model is appropriate for the specific task at hand. Different AI models have distinct strengths and weaknesses, and selecting the right model depends on the nature of the problem and the data available. In this section, we explore the key considerations for evaluating model suitability for specific tasks.

a) **Task Requirements:** The first step in evaluating model suitability is to clearly define the task requirements. Determine the nature of the problem, whether it is a classification, regression, clustering, or other types of tasks. Understanding the expected output and performance metrics is essential to guide the selection process.

b) **Data Characteristics:** Examine the data characteristics, such as data type, structure, and dimensionality. Consider the size of the dataset, the presence of missing values or outliers, and the distribution of classes or labels. Different AI models have varying data requirements, and the model should be able to handle the data effectively.

c) **Model Complexity:** Assess the complexity of the problem. Simple problems may be adequately addressed by traditional Machine Learning algorithms, such as decision trees or logistic regression. For more complex problems with non-linear relationships, Deep Learning models like neural networks may be more appropriate.

d) **Interpretability:** Consider the importance of model interpretability for the task. In some domains, such as healthcare or finance, interpretability is critical for understanding the reasoning behind model predictions. In such cases, simpler models like decision trees or linear models may be preferred.

e) **Performance Requirements:** Determine the performance requirements for the task. Consider factors like prediction accuracy, precision, recall, or area under the curve (AUC) for classification tasks, and mean squared error (MSE) or mean absolute error (MAE) for regression tasks. Some tasks may prioritize model robustness over achieving the highest accuracy.

f) **Data Availability:** Evaluate the availability of data for model training. Deep Learning models, particularly those with millions of parameters, may require significant amounts of data for effective training. If data is limited, simpler Machine Learning models may be a better choice.

g) **Computation Resources:** Consider the computational resources available for model training and inference. Deep Learning models, especially large neural networks, demand substantial computational power and may not be feasible without access to GPUs or TPUs. Machine Learning models are generally more computationally efficient.

h) **Previous Successes:** Review past successes in similar tasks and domains. Knowledge of successful AI models and techniques for similar problems can provide valuable insights into which models are more likely to succeed.

i) **Ensemble Approaches:** For critical tasks, consider using ensemble approaches that combine predictions from multiple models. Ensemble methods like bagging and boosting can improve prediction accuracy and robustness.

j) **Experimentation and Evaluation:** Perform rigorous experimentation and evaluation of different models. Use techniques like cross-validation and hyperparameter tuning to objectively compare the performance of various models on the specific task.

Conclusion: Evaluating model suitability for specific tasks is a multifaceted process that requires a deep understanding of the problem, data, and performance requirements. By considering factors like task requirements, data characteristics, model complexity, interpretability, and resource constraints, AI consultants can identify the most suitable AI model for the task at hand. Rigorous experimentation and evaluation help ensure that the selected model aligns with client objectives and delivers valuable AI solutions that drive business impact.

6.3 Implementing and Fine-Tuning AI Models

After selecting the most suitable AI model for a specific task, the next crucial step in AI consulting is implementing and fine-tuning the chosen model. Implementation involves building the AI model using programming frameworks and libraries, while fine-tuning focuses on optimizing the model's performance and parameters. In this section, we explore the key steps and best practices for implementing and fine-tuning AI models.

Model Implementation:

The implementation process involves translating the selected AI model from the theoretical description into a functional software application. The following steps are typically involved:

a) **Selecting Programming Frameworks:** Choose appropriate programming frameworks and libraries that support the selected AI model. For instance, TensorFlow and PyTorch are popular choices for implementing Deep Learning models, while Scikit-learn is commonly used for traditional Machine Learning algorithms.

b) **Data Integration:** Preprocess and integrate the data, ensuring it is in a suitable format for model training and testing. Follow the data preprocessing steps identified earlier in the consulting process.

c) **Building the Model Architecture:** Define the architecture of the AI model, specifying the number of layers, nodes, and activation functions for neural networks or the parameters for traditional Machine Learning algorithms.

d) **Model Training:** Use the training data to fit the model to the data, adjusting the model's parameters to minimize the chosen loss or error function. This process may require multiple iterations and epochs, especially for Deep Learning models.

e) **Hyperparameter Tuning:** Fine-tuning the model involves optimizing hyperparameters to achieve better performance. Hyperparameters are parameters that are not learned during training but set before the training process. Techniques like grid search, random search, or Bayesian optimization are used to search for the best combination of hyperparameters that maximize the model's performance.

f) **Regularization:** Regularization techniques are employed to prevent overfitting, a situation where the model performs well on the training data but poorly on new, unseen data. Common regularization techniques include L1 and L2 regularization for neural networks and dropout for Deep Learning models.

g) **Early Stopping:** Early stopping is a technique used to prevent overfitting. During training, the model's performance on a validation set is monitored, and training is stopped when the performance starts to degrade, indicating overfitting.

h) **Transfer Learning (for Deep Learning Models):** Transfer learning is an approach that involves using a pre-trained model as a starting point and fine-tuning it for a different task or dataset. This approach is particularly useful when working with limited data, as it leverages knowledge from a related task to boost performance.

i) **Model Evaluation:** After implementing and fine-tuning the model, it is crucial to evaluate its performance on a separate test dataset. Use appropriate evaluation metrics, such as accuracy, precision, recall, F1-score, or mean squared error, depending on the nature of the task.

j) **Model Deployment:** Once the AI model meets the desired performance criteria, it is ready for deployment. Depending on the application, the model can be integrated into existing software systems, cloud services, mobile applications, or edge devices.

Conclusion: Implementing and fine-tuning AI models are critical stages in AI consulting that bridge the gap between theoretical concepts and practical applications. By selecting suitable programming frameworks, preprocessing data, building the model architecture, and optimizing hyperparameters, AI consultants ensure that the AI model performs effectively on the specific task. Rigorous evaluation and fine-tuning processes lead to robust and accurate AI solutions that align with client objectives and deliver significant business value.

Chapter 7: AI Model Evaluation and Validation

In AI consulting, evaluating the performance and robustness of AI models is essential to ensure the reliability and fairness of the solutions delivered to clients. Chapter 7 delves into the realm of performance metrics, cross-validation, and techniques for ensuring model robustness and fairness. As AI consultants, understanding these topics empowers you to deliver AI solutions that meet high standards of accuracy, generalization, and ethical considerations. Let's explore the first three topics covered in this chapter:

7.1 Performance Metrics for AI Models:

Measuring the effectiveness of AI models requires a careful selection of performance metrics. In this section, we explore a wide range of metrics used in different AI domains. For classification tasks, we discuss accuracy, precision, recall, F1-score, and ROC-AUC. In regression tasks, we delve into metrics like mean squared error (MSE) and mean absolute error (MAE). Moreover, we discuss the importance of domain-specific metrics to assess the AI model's performance in real-world scenarios.

7.2 Cross-Validation and Testing Techniques:

Overfitting and underfitting are common challenges in AI model development. Cross-validation is a powerful technique used to assess a model's generalization capabilities and mitigate these issues. In this section, we explore various cross-validation methods, including k-fold cross-validation and leave-one-out cross-validation. We also discuss the importance of testing data, validation sets, and model selection based on cross-validation results.

7.3 Ensuring Model Robustness and Fairness:

AI models must be robust and perform consistently across diverse scenarios. In this section, we delve into techniques to enhance model robustness, such as data augmentation, transfer learning, and adversarial testing. Moreover, we discuss the critical issue of fairness in AI models and explore methodologies to identify and mitigate biases. AI consultants learn how to assess model fairness using metrics like disparate impact and equal opportunity.

Conclusion: Through comprehensive evaluation techniques, AI consultants can fine-tune AI models to deliver solutions that align with the clients' objectives and expectations. We emphasize the significance of model fairness in promoting ethical

AI practices and ensuring AI solutions do not perpetuate biases or discriminate against specific groups. By mastering model evaluation and fairness considerations, AI consultants can confidently deliver high-impact, reliable, and equitable AI solutions that drive transformative value for their clients.

7.1 Performance Metrics for AI Models

Performance metrics are essential tools used to evaluate the effectiveness of AI models in AI consulting. These metrics quantify how well the models perform on specific tasks and help AI consultants make informed decisions regarding model selection, fine-tuning, and deployment. In this section, we explore some of the key performance metrics commonly used for different types of AI tasks.

Classification Tasks:

In classification tasks, AI models predict the class or category to which an input belongs. Common performance metrics for classification tasks include:

1. **Accuracy:** The proportion of correctly classified instances to the total number of instances in the dataset. It provides an overall measure of model performance.

2. **Precision:** The proportion of true positive predictions (correctly identified positive cases) to the total number of positive predictions. It measures the accuracy of positive predictions.

3. **Recall (Sensitivity or True Positive Rate):** The proportion of true positive predictions to the total number of actual positive instances. It measures the model's ability to correctly identify positive cases.

4. **F1-Score:** The harmonic mean of precision and recall. It balances precision and recall when dealing with imbalanced datasets.

5. **Area Under the Receiver Operating Characteristic Curve (AUC-ROC):** It measures the model's ability to distinguish between positive and negative classes across different thresholds.

Regression Tasks:

In regression tasks, AI models predict a continuous numerical value. Common performance metrics for regression tasks include:

1. **Mean Squared Error (MSE):** The average of squared differences between predicted and actual values. It penalizes large prediction errors.

2. **Mean Absolute Error (MAE):** The average of absolute differences between predicted and actual values. It provides a measure of the model's accuracy without squaring the errors.

3. **R-squared (Coefficient of Determination):** It measures the proportion of the variance in the target variable that is predictable from the input features. A higher R-squared indicates a better fit of the model to the data.

Clustering Tasks:

In clustering tasks, AI models group data points into clusters based on similarity. Since clustering is an unsupervised learning task, performance metrics differ from classification and regression tasks. Commonly used metrics for clustering tasks include:

a) **Silhouette Score:** Measures how similar an instance is to its own cluster compared to other clusters. A higher silhouette score indicates better-defined clusters.

b) **Davies-Bouldin Index:** Measures the average similarity between each cluster and its most similar cluster. Lower values indicate better clustering.

Natural Language Processing (NLP) Tasks:

In NLP tasks, AI models process and understand human language. Performance metrics for NLP tasks depend on the specific application and may include metrics like accuracy, precision, recall, or BLEU score (for machine translation tasks).

Computer Vision Tasks:

In computer vision tasks, AI models process and interpret visual data, such as images and videos. Performance metrics depend on the task, such as accuracy for image classification or Intersection over Union (IoU) for object detection and segmentation tasks.

Conclusion: Performance metrics play a crucial role in AI consulting to objectively assess AI model performance. The choice of metrics depends on the task at hand, whether it's classification, regression, clustering, NLP, or computer vision. AI consultants use these metrics to fine-tune models, compare different algorithms, and make data-driven decisions to deliver accurate and reliable AI solutions that meet client objectives.

7.2 Cross-Validation and Testing Techniques

In AI consulting, cross-validation and testing techniques are essential for assessing the performance of AI models and ensuring their generalization capabilities. These techniques involve dividing the data into subsets for training, validation, and testing, allowing AI consultants to obtain reliable performance estimates and make informed decisions about model selection and fine-tuning. In this section, we explore cross-validation and testing techniques commonly used in AI consulting.

Cross-Validation:

Cross-validation is a resampling technique used to evaluate the model's performance on limited data. It involves dividing the dataset into multiple subsets or folds. The model is trained on a combination of these folds and tested on the remaining fold. This process is repeated multiple times, ensuring that each fold serves as both a training and testing set. Common types of cross-validation include:

a) **k-Fold Cross-Validation:** The dataset is divided into k subsets (or folds). The model is trained on k-1 folds and tested on the remaining fold. This process is repeated k times, with each fold serving as the test set once.

b) **Stratified k-Fold Cross-Validation:** This is an extension of k-fold cross-validation that maintains the class distribution in each fold, making it particularly useful for imbalanced datasets.

c) **Leave-One-Out Cross-Validation (LOOCV):** Each data point is used as a test set, and the model is trained on all other data points. This is computationally expensive but provides a robust estimate, especially for small datasets.

d) **Hold-Out Validation:** Hold-out validation is a simple technique where the dataset is split into two subsets: a training set and a test set. The model is trained on the training set and evaluated on the test set. While easy to implement, hold-out validation may lead to higher variance in the performance estimate, especially with small datasets.

e) **Time Series Split:** For time series data, where the temporal order is crucial, a time series split is used. The data is split based on time, ensuring that the model is trained on past data and tested on future data, mimicking real-world scenarios.

f) **Nested Cross-Validation:** Nested cross-validation is used for hyperparameter tuning. It involves performing cross-validation within cross-validation loops to select the best hyperparameters for the model.

g) **Train-Validation-Test Split:** In this technique, the dataset is divided into three subsets: training, validation, and test sets. The model is trained on the training set, hyperparameters are tuned using the validation set, and the final performance is evaluated on the test set.

h) **Bootstrapping:** Bootstrapping is a resampling technique where multiple datasets are created by randomly sampling with replacement from the original dataset. Models are trained and tested on these bootstrapped datasets to estimate performance variability.

Conclusion: Cross-validation and testing techniques are essential tools in AI consulting to evaluate AI model performance and make data-driven decisions. By employing techniques like k-fold cross-validation, hold-out validation, time series split, and nested cross-validation, AI consultants obtain reliable performance estimates and ensure that the selected models generalize well to new, unseen data. Rigorous evaluation using appropriate validation techniques leads to accurate and robust AI solutions that deliver valuable insights and drive business success for clients.

7.3 Ensuring Model Robustness and Fairness

In AI consulting, ensuring model robustness and fairness is of paramount importance to build reliable and ethical AI solutions. Model robustness refers to the ability of an AI model to perform well across different datasets and in real-world scenarios. Fairness, on the other hand, addresses the need to prevent biased outcomes and discriminatory behavior in AI models. In this section, we explore the key considerations and best practices to achieve model robustness and fairness in AI consulting.

a) **Data Quality and Diversity:** To ensure model robustness, AI consultants must work with high-quality and diverse datasets. High-quality data minimizes errors and inconsistencies, while diverse data represents various scenarios that the model may encounter in the real world. Ensuring data diversity helps prevent biases and ensures that the model is exposed to a wide range of examples during training.

b) **Cross-Validation and Performance Evaluation:** Performing cross-validation and rigorous performance evaluation on different subsets of data helps assess the model's robustness. If the model consistently performs well across different folds and datasets, it is more likely to generalize effectively.

c) **Regular Model Maintenance and Updates:** AI models may become less effective over time as data distributions change. Regularly monitoring the model's performance and updating it with fresh data is crucial to maintain its accuracy and robustness.

d) **Addressing Biases:** Addressing biases in AI models is essential to ensure fairness. AI consultants must carefully examine the data used for training to identify potential biases and take corrective measures. Techniques like re-sampling, re-weighting, and fairness-aware learning can be employed to mitigate biases.

e) **Fairness Metrics:** AI consultants should use fairness metrics to evaluate model fairness across different subgroups in the data, such as race, gender, or age. Common fairness metrics include disparate impact, equal opportunity, and equalized odds.

f) **Interpretability and Explainability:** Interpretable and explainable AI models help identify potential biases and make them more transparent. Techniques like Local Interpretable Model-Agnostic Explanations (LIME) and SHapley Additive exPlanations (SHAP) can provide insights into how the model arrives at its decisions.

g) **Regular Fairness Audits:** Regular fairness audits are essential to monitor the model's performance for fairness over time. Conducting fairness audits helps identify any biases that may emerge during model deployment and make necessary adjustments.

h) **Collaboration with Domain Experts:** Collaborating with domain experts, ethicists, and stakeholders is vital to understand the potential ethical implications of the AI model and ensure that the model's objectives align with ethical guidelines and societal norms.

Conclusion: Ensuring model robustness and fairness is a continuous process in AI consulting. By working with high-quality and diverse data, performing cross-validation, and regularly updating the model, consultants can enhance model robustness. Addressing biases, using fairness metrics, and ensuring interpretability promote model fairness and reduce discriminatory outcomes. Collaboration with domain experts and stakeholders helps create ethical and responsible AI solutions that deliver reliable insights and drive positive business impact. Striving for model robustness and fairness is not only a professional responsibility but also an ethical imperative to build AI systems that benefit society as a whole.

Chapter 8: Deployment and Integration

Deploying AI solutions into existing systems is a critical phase in AI consulting, as it bridges the gap between development and real-world implementation. Chapter 8 explores the intricacies of integrating AI solutions, handling deployment challenges, and ensuring seamless post-deployment monitoring and maintenance. As AI consultants, mastering these aspects is essential to deliver robust and sustainable AI solutions that drive continuous value. Let's explore the first three topics covered in this chapter:

8.1 Integrating AI Solutions into Existing Systems:

AI solutions must seamlessly integrate with clients' existing systems and workflows to maximize their impact. In this section, we discuss the importance of compatibility and interoperability when deploying AI models. AI consultants learn strategies for integrating AI solutions into diverse environments, including cloud-based systems, mobile applications, and enterprise infrastructures. The focus is on minimizing disruption and ensuring a smooth transition for end-users.

8.2 Handling Deployment Challenges:

The deployment phase can present unexpected challenges that AI consultants must address proactively. This section covers potential deployment challenges, such as hardware limitations, data inconsistencies, and model versioning. Consultants will learn how to devise contingency plans and collaborate with stakeholders to tackle deployment hurdles effectively.

8.3 Post-Deployment Monitoring and Maintenance:

AI solutions require ongoing monitoring and maintenance to ensure their performance remains optimal over time. In this section, we explore techniques for tracking AI model performance, detecting drift, and implementing feedback loops. AI consultants will gain insights into conducting periodic model retraining and version updates to keep AI solutions up-to-date and relevant.

Conclusion: Throughout this chapter, we emphasize the importance of open communication with clients and end-users during the deployment process. By actively addressing concerns and providing comprehensive support, AI consultants can build trust and facilitate the successful adoption of AI solutions. As AI models integrate into real-world systems, consultants must be prepared to handle challenges and adapt to evolving requirements. By mastering the deployment and maintenance phase, AI consultants can ensure long-term success and deliver AI solutions that consistently deliver value and drive transformative impact for their clients.

8.1 Integrating AI Solutions into Existing Systems

a) **Infrastructure Requirements:** AI consultants start by understanding the client's infrastructure and technical requirements. They assess the hardware, software, and network capabilities necessary to support the AI model's deployment. This includes considerations for scalability, computational resources, and data storage.

b) **Model Optimization:** Before deployment, AI models may require optimization to ensure efficient inference and reduce computational overhead. Techniques like quantization, pruning, and model compression can be applied to reduce the model's size and improve its execution speed.

c) **Deployment Options:** AI models can be deployed in various environments, such as on-premises, cloud, edge devices, or hybrid setups. Consultants work with the client to determine the best deployment option based on factors like data privacy, latency requirements, and cost considerations.

d) **API Design:** For AI models accessed through APIs, consultants design robust and user-friendly APIs that encapsulate the model's functionality. Well-defined APIs make it easier for developers to integrate the AI solution into their applications.

e) **Versioning and Monitoring:** Consultants implement version control for deployed models, enabling easy rollbacks and updates. They also set up monitoring and logging mechanisms to track the model's performance and detect any issues that may arise during real-world usage.

f) **DevOps Integration:** Integrating AI solutions into the client's DevOps pipeline is essential for smooth development, testing, and deployment processes. Consultants collaborate with the client's DevOps team to ensure that AI models fit seamlessly into existing workflows.

g) **Continuous Integration and Continuous Deployment (CI/CD):** CI/CD practices streamline the deployment process, enabling automatic testing and deployment of model updates. Consultants set up CI/CD pipelines to ensure that the latest models are continuously deployed while maintaining the required quality standards.

h) **Security and Privacy:** Security and data privacy are critical considerations during deployment. AI consultants implement security measures, such as encryption and access controls, to protect sensitive data and prevent unauthorized access.

i) **User Interface and Experience:** For AI solutions with user interfaces, consultants design intuitive and user-friendly interfaces that allow users to interact with the AI model effectively. A well-designed user interface enhances the overall user experience.

j) **Documentation and Support:** Comprehensive documentation is essential for clients and developers to understand how to use and integrate the AI solution. Consultants provide documentation, tutorials, and support to ensure that users can make the most of the AI model's capabilities.

Conclusion: Chapter 8 focuses on the deployment and integration phase of AI consulting, where AI models are put into action to deliver value to clients. By understanding infrastructure requirements, optimizing models, and offering flexible deployment options, consultants ensure that AI solutions fit seamlessly into the client's ecosystem. Continuous integration, monitoring, and support ensure that the deployed models maintain high performance over time. Prioritizing security, privacy, and user experience builds trust and enhances the adoption of AI solutions among end-users. Ultimately, successful deployment and integration lead to real-world impact and positive outcomes for clients, transforming businesses through the power of AI.

8.2 Handling Deployment Challenges

Deploying AI solutions comes with its set of challenges, and AI consultants must be prepared to tackle them to ensure the success of the deployment. In this section, we explore some common deployment challenges in AI consulting and strategies to address them effectively.

Data Compatibility and Quality:

Challenge: AI models often require specific data formats, and inconsistencies in data quality can affect model performance during deployment.

Strategy: Data preprocessing and data quality checks are crucial before deployment. AI consultants should work closely with the client's data team to ensure that the data is compatible with the model and meets the required quality standards.

Model Interpretability:

Challenge: Complex AI models, such as Deep Learning neural networks, can lack interpretability, making it challenging to explain their decisions to stakeholders.

Strategy: Employ techniques for model interpretability, such as LIME and SHAP, to generate human-readable explanations for individual predictions. Explainable AI helps build trust and ensures the model's transparency.

Resource Constraints:

Challenge: In edge computing or resource-limited environments, deploying resource-intensive AI models can be challenging.

Strategy: Optimize the model's size and computational requirements through techniques like model quantization, pruning, and model compression. This reduces the model's footprint while maintaining acceptable performance.

Real-Time Inference:

Challenge: Some AI applications require real-time or low-latency inference, making it crucial to minimize prediction times.

Strategy: Optimize the model and deployment environment to achieve low-latency inference. Techniques like model quantization and using hardware accelerators (e.g., GPUs, TPUs) can speed up inference.

Scalability:

Challenge: Scalability becomes an issue when deploying AI models to handle a large number of concurrent requests.

Strategy: Deploy AI models on cloud platforms that provide auto-scaling capabilities. This ensures that the infrastructure automatically adjusts to handle varying workloads.

Security and Privacy:

Challenge: AI models can be vulnerable to security breaches and may process sensitive data, raising concerns about data privacy.

Strategy: Implement robust security measures, such as encryption, access controls, and secure APIs. Follow industry best practices for data handling to protect sensitive information.

Model Drift:

Challenge: Model drift occurs when the model's performance degrades over time due to changes in data distributions.

Strategy: Set up monitoring mechanisms to detect model drift and regularly retrain the model with new data to maintain its accuracy.

Integration Complexity:

Challenge: Integrating AI solutions into existing software systems can be complex and may require modifications to the existing codebase.

Strategy: Work closely with the client's development team to understand the system architecture and design APIs that seamlessly integrate the AI model with the existing infrastructure.

User Acceptance:

Challenge: Users may be resistant to adopting AI solutions, especially if they perceive them as black-box systems.

Strategy: Provide thorough training and education to end-users on how to use the AI solution effectively. Transparent communication about the benefits and limitations of the AI model can also improve user acceptance.

Conclusion: Handling deployment challenges is an integral part of AI consulting. By proactively addressing data compatibility and quality issues, ensuring model interpretability, optimizing for resource constraints, and addressing scalability and security concerns, AI consultants can overcome deployment challenges effectively. Continuous monitoring, addressing model drift, and streamlining integration processes ensure that AI solutions deliver value over the long term. By prioritizing user acceptance and providing support throughout the deployment phase, consultants can ensure the successful adoption and utilization of AI solutions, leading to positive outcomes for clients and their businesses.

8.3 Post-Deployment Monitoring and Maintenance

In AI consulting, post-deployment monitoring and maintenance are critical to ensuring that AI solutions continue to perform effectively and deliver value to clients. AI models deployed in real-world environments may encounter new challenges and changes over time, necessitating ongoing monitoring and updates. In this section, we explore the importance of post-deployment monitoring and maintenance and the best practices to ensure the long-term success of AI solutions.

a) **Performance Monitoring:** Post-deployment, AI consultants continuously monitor the performance of deployed models to detect any degradation in accuracy or other performance metrics. Monitoring includes tracking key performance indicators and conducting regular assessments to identify potential issues.

b) **Model Drift Detection:** Model drift can occur when the data distribution of the real-world environment changes over time, causing the model's performance to deteriorate. Consultants implement drift detection mechanisms to identify when model updates are required to maintain accuracy.

c) **Data Quality Monitoring:** Data quality is essential for AI model performance. Consultants continually assess data quality to ensure that the model's input data remains accurate, relevant, and representative of the real-world scenarios.

d) **Security and Privacy Audits:** Regular security and privacy audits are crucial to safeguard sensitive data and prevent security breaches. Consultants assess potential vulnerabilities and ensure that the deployed AI solutions adhere to security and privacy standards.

e) **Regular Model Updates:** To maintain the model's effectiveness, consultants schedule regular model updates to incorporate new data and adapt to changing environments. This includes retraining the model with fresh data to ensure it remains up-to-date.

f) **Feedback Collection and Analysis:** Collecting feedback from end-users and stakeholders is essential to understand how the AI solution is performing in practical scenarios. Consultants analyze feedback to identify areas for improvement and potential user concerns.

g) **Version Control and Rollbacks:** Version control ensures that different iterations of the model and its components are managed efficiently. Consultants can roll back to previous versions if necessary, especially when deploying new updates.

h) **Scalability Monitoring:** As the demand for AI solutions grows, scalability becomes crucial. Monitoring system performance and scaling capabilities help consultants adjust resources accordingly.

i) **Documentation and Knowledge Transfer:** Thorough documentation of the AI solution, its components, and the deployment process is essential for future maintenance and knowledge transfer. It facilitates seamless collaboration among team members and ensures continuity.

j) **Collaboration with Domain Experts:** Continuing collaboration with domain experts and stakeholders is vital to stay informed about changes in requirements and potential challenges faced during deployment. Regular communication ensures that the AI solution remains relevant and aligned with business goals.

Conclusion:
Post-deployment monitoring and maintenance are integral to the success of AI consulting projects. By continuously monitoring performance, detecting model drift, and maintaining data quality, AI consultants ensure that the deployed AI solutions deliver reliable and accurate results. Regular updates, security audits, and version control contribute to the longevity of AI models. Collaboration with stakeholders and the collection of user feedback help consultants adapt to changing

requirements and ensure user satisfaction. By prioritizing post-deployment monitoring and maintenance, AI consultants contribute to the sustained success of AI solutions and their positive impact on clients' businesses.

Part 3: Mastering the Soft Skills

In AI consulting, technical expertise alone is not enough to succeed. Mastering soft skills is equally crucial for AI consultants to effectively communicate, collaborate, and build strong relationships with clients and team members. Part 3 focuses on developing and honing the essential soft skills required for a successful career in AI consulting. This section explores the key soft skills and their significance in the consulting process.

a) **Communication Skills:** Effective communication is the foundation of successful consulting. AI consultants must be able to explain complex technical concepts to non-technical stakeholders in a clear and concise manner. Active listening is equally important to understand client requirements and concerns.

b) **Problem-Solving and Critical Thinking:** AI consultants encounter various challenges during projects. Developing strong problem-solving and critical thinking skills enables consultants to analyze issues, devise creative solutions, and make informed decisions.

c) **Adaptability and Flexibility:** The AI landscape is constantly evolving, and projects may face unexpected changes. Being adaptable and flexible allows AI consultants to respond quickly to new requirements, technologies, and business environments.

d) **Empathy and Emotional Intelligence:** Understanding and empathizing with clients' needs and concerns build trust and rapport. Emotional intelligence helps AI consultants navigate difficult situations, manage conflicts, and foster positive relationships.

e) **Collaboration and Teamwork:** AI projects involve multidisciplinary teams, including data scientists, engineers, and domain experts. Strong collaboration and teamwork skills enable consultants to work harmoniously, leverage diverse expertise, and deliver holistic solutions.

f) **Client Relationship Management:** Building and maintaining strong client relationships are essential for successful AI consulting. Consultants must prioritize client satisfaction, address their feedback, and actively seek to understand their business objectives.

g) **Time Management:** AI projects often have tight deadlines and require efficient time management. Effective prioritization and organization of tasks help consultants meet project milestones and deliverables.

h) **Presentation and Public Speaking:** Presenting findings, results, and recommendations is a vital aspect of AI consulting. Developing strong presentation and public speaking skills allows consultants to convey information confidently and persuasively.

i) **Negotiation and Persuasion:** During project discussions, consultants may need to negotiate with clients or stakeholders on various aspects. Persuasion skills help consultants communicate the value of their recommendations and gain buy-in from decision-makers.

j) **Continuous Learning:** AI is a rapidly evolving field, and staying updated with the latest advancements is essential for AI consultants. A commitment to continuous learning helps consultants remain at the forefront of AI technologies and methodologies.

Conclusion:
Part 3 emphasizes the significance of mastering soft skills in AI consulting. By developing effective communication, problem-solving, and adaptability, consultants can navigate challenges and build strong client relationships. Empathy, collaboration, and emotional intelligence foster positive interactions and teamwork within projects. Time management, presentation, and negotiation skills contribute to the successful delivery of AI solutions. A commitment to continuous learning ensures that consultants stay informed about the latest developments in AI. By combining technical expertise with strong soft skills, AI consultants elevate their consulting capabilities, enhance client satisfaction, and drive impactful business outcomes.

Chapter 9: Communication and Client Management

AI consulting goes beyond technical expertise; it requires a strong set of soft skills to effectively communicate with clients, stakeholders, and team members. Chapter 9 explores the art of effective communication, presenting complex AI concepts to non-technical stakeholders, and building and maintaining client relationships. As AI consultants, honing these soft skills is instrumental in fostering collaboration, understanding clients' needs, and ensuring the successful execution of AI projects. Let's explore the first three topics covered in this chapter:

9.1 Effective Communication Strategies:

Effective communication is the cornerstone of successful AI consulting. In this section, we delve into communication techniques that help AI consultants convey complex ideas with clarity and precision. This includes active listening, asking clarifying questions, and using visual aids to enhance understanding. Additionally, we explore methods to tailor communication styles to different audiences, ensuring that technical and non-technical stakeholders comprehend the AI consulting process.

9.2 Presenting Complex AI Concepts to Non-Technical Stakeholders:

AI consultants often find themselves presenting intricate AI concepts to stakeholders who may not have a technical background. This section provides strategies to distill complex AI topics into digestible and relatable information. Consultants will learn how to craft compelling narratives, use storytelling techniques, and emphasize real-world impact to engage non-technical stakeholders and secure buy-in for AI projects.

9.3 Building and Maintaining Client Relationships:

Strong client relationships are essential for repeat business and positive referrals. In this section, we discuss the art of building rapport with clients, understanding their unique needs, and delivering exceptional service. AI consultants will learn to manage expectations, provide regular updates, and demonstrate the value of AI solutions to maintain long-term client partnerships. Additionally, we explore strategies for handling challenges and resolving conflicts to nurture positive and collaborative relationships.

Conclusion: Throughout this chapter, we emphasize empathy and adaptability as crucial attributes in AI consulting. By cultivating effective communication and presentation skills, AI consultants can build trust, enhance project outcomes, and foster positive working relationships with clients and stakeholders. The ability to convey complex AI concepts in a relatable manner is a testament to the consultant's expertise and dedication to ensuring AI solutions meet clients' specific goals. With mastery of soft skills, AI consultants elevate their consulting practice to new heights of success and impact.

9.1 Effective Communication Strategies

Effective communication is a cornerstone of success in AI consulting. Clear and concise communication helps AI consultants convey complex technical concepts, understand client needs, and foster productive relationships. In this section, we explore essential communication strategies that enhance AI consultants' abilities to deliver value to clients and work effectively with team members.

a) **Tailor Communication to the Audience:** Adapt the level of technical detail and language used in communication to suit the audience. Non-technical stakeholders may require explanations in simple terms, while technical experts may need more in-depth discussions.

b) **Use Visual Aids and Data Visualization:** Visual aids, such as charts, graphs, and infographics, help illustrate data insights and findings effectively. Data visualization techniques enhance understanding and make complex information more accessible.

c) **Practice Active Listening:** Listen actively to clients, team members, and stakeholders. Understand their perspectives, concerns, and requirements. Active listening fosters better understanding and shows respect for others' opinions.

d) **Be Clear and Concise:** In written and verbal communication, be clear and concise. Avoid jargon and use straightforward language to ensure the message is easily understood.

e) **Use Real-World Examples:** Use real-world examples and analogies to illustrate technical concepts. Relating AI concepts to familiar scenarios helps stakeholders grasp the relevance and potential impact.

f) **Be Transparent and Honest:** Transparency is crucial in communication. Be honest about project progress, challenges, and potential limitations of the AI solution. Trust is built through open and candid communication.

g) **Provide Regular Updates:** Keep clients and stakeholders informed about project progress with regular updates. Share successes, milestones, and any deviations from the initial plan promptly.

h) **Clarify Expectations:** Clearly articulate project goals, deliverables, and timelines to set clear expectations from the beginning. Review and reiterate the agreed-upon expectations periodically.

i) **Anticipate Questions:** Anticipate potential questions and concerns that clients or team members may have and proactively address them in communication. Being prepared shows foresight and professionalism.

j) **Be Respectful and Empathetic:** Respect the viewpoints and perspectives of others, even in the face of disagreement. Practice empathy by considering others' feelings and experiences when communicating.

k) **Seek Feedback:** Encourage feedback from clients and team members. Actively seek input on how communication can be improved to meet their needs better.

l) **Use Collaborative Language:** Use collaborative language that promotes a sense of teamwork and partnership. Phrases like "we can work together to" or "let's explore options" encourage collaboration and cooperation.

Conclusion: Effective communication is a fundamental skill that empowers AI consultants to build strong relationships with clients, understand their needs, and deliver impactful solutions. By tailoring communication to the audience, using visual aids, and practicing active listening, consultants can ensure that technical information is conveyed clearly and comprehensively. Transparency, regular updates, and respect foster trust and rapport with stakeholders. Seeking feedback and using collaborative language create a supportive and productive environment for teamwork. Implementing these effective communication strategies enhances AI consulting endeavors, leading to successful project outcomes and positive client experiences.

9.2 Presenting Complex AI Concepts to Non-Technical Stakeholders

Communicating complex AI concepts to non-technical stakeholders is a crucial skill in AI consulting. Non-technical audiences may lack familiarity with AI terminology and may find technical jargon overwhelming. Therefore, AI consultants must be adept at conveying technical information in a clear and understandable manner. Here are some strategies for presenting complex AI concepts to non-technical stakeholders effectively:

a) **Know Your Audience:** Understand the background and expertise of your audience. Tailor your presentation to suit their level of technical understanding. Avoid using overly technical language and focus on conveying the essential points.

b) **Use Analogies and Metaphors:** Use familiar analogies and metaphors to explain complex AI concepts. Relating AI processes to everyday scenarios helps non-technical stakeholders grasp the relevance and impact of AI in their context.

c) **Start with the Why:** Begin your presentation by explaining why the AI solution is relevant to the stakeholders' business objectives. Highlight the potential benefits and impact of the AI solution to capture their interest from the start.

d) **Visualize Data and Results:** Utilize data visualization techniques to present AI findings visually. Charts, graphs, and infographics can help make complex data more accessible and easier to understand.

e) **Provide Real-World Examples:** Use real-world examples to illustrate the practical applications of AI concepts. Demonstrating how AI has solved similar challenges in other industries or use cases can make the benefits tangible to stakeholders.

f) **Focus on High-Level Insights:** Avoid overwhelming non-technical stakeholders with technical details. Instead, focus on providing high-level insights and key takeaways from the AI analysis. Summarize complex findings in simple and understandable terms.

g) **Prepare Engaging Presentations:** Craft engaging and well-structured presentations that flow logically. Use storytelling techniques to maintain stakeholders' interest and emphasize the relevance of AI in achieving their business goals.

h) **Address Concerns and Questions:** Be prepared to address concerns and questions that stakeholders may have. Anticipate common queries and provide clear and concise responses to put their minds at ease.

i) **Offer Hands-On Demonstrations:** If possible, provide hands-on demonstrations of the AI solution. Interactive demonstrations allow stakeholders to see the AI solution in action and gain a deeper understanding of its capabilities.

j) **Seek Feedback and Encourage Questions:** Invite feedback from non-technical stakeholders and encourage them to ask questions during and after the presentation. Demonstrating openness to feedback and curiosity encourages a collaborative atmosphere.

Conclusion:
Presenting complex AI concepts to non-technical stakeholders is a critical skill that AI consultants must master in AI consulting. By understanding their audience, using analogies and real-world examples, visualizing data, and focusing on high-level insights, consultants can effectively communicate the value of AI solutions to non-technical stakeholders. Engaging presentations, hands-on demonstrations, and transparent communication foster understanding and build trust with stakeholders. Through these strategies, AI consultants bridge the gap between technical expertise and non-technical audiences, leading to successful AI implementations and positive business outcomes.

9.3 Building and Maintaining Client Relationships

In AI consulting, building and maintaining strong client relationships are essential for long-term success and repeat business. Positive client relationships lead to trust, open communication, and successful collaborations. Here are some strategies to build and maintain client relationships effectively:

a) **Understand Client Needs:** Take the time to understand your client's business objectives, challenges, and expectations. Actively listen to their needs and concerns, and tailor your AI solutions to address their specific requirements.

b) **Be Transparent and Honest:** Transparency and honesty are key to building trust with clients. Be upfront about the scope of the project, potential limitations, and any challenges that may arise. Keep clients informed about project progress and changes.

c) **Communicate Effectively:** Maintain clear and open communication with clients throughout the project. Provide regular updates, respond promptly to inquiries, and be accessible to address concerns or feedback.

d) **Exceed Expectations:** Go the extra mile to deliver value to your clients. Exceeding expectations demonstrates your commitment to their success and reinforces the client's confidence in your expertise.

e) **Offer Personalized Solutions:** Tailor your AI solutions to meet the unique needs of each client. Avoid using a one-size-fits-all approach and instead, develop customized solutions that align with their business goals.

f) **Seek Feedback:** Actively seek feedback from clients about their experience working with your AI solutions. Use their feedback to continuously improve your services and address any areas of concern.

g) **Be Responsive and Reliable:** Be responsive to client inquiries and requests. Demonstrating reliability and attentiveness shows that you value their time and are committed to their success.

h) **Celebrate Milestones:** Celebrate project milestones and achievements with your clients. Acknowledge their contributions and demonstrate appreciation for their partnership.

i) **Foster Long-Term Relationships:** Focus on building long-term relationships rather than one-off transactions. By showing your commitment to their success over the long term, clients are more likely to trust and invest in your services.

j) **Provide Exceptional Support:** Offer ongoing support even after the project is completed. Be available to address any post-project questions or issues that may arise.

k) **Continuously Learn and Improve:** Stay up-to-date with the latest advancements in AI and continuously improve your skills and knowledge. Clients value consultants who are at the forefront of the field.

l) **Be Professional and Respectful:** Maintain a professional and respectful demeanor in all interactions with clients. Treat them as valued partners and collaborators.

Conclusion: Building and maintaining client relationships is a critical aspect of AI consulting. By understanding client needs, communicating effectively, and being transparent and honest, consultants can build trust and rapport with clients. Offering personalized solutions, exceeding expectations, and providing exceptional support demonstrate commitment to client success. By fostering long-term relationships and continuously improving skills, AI consultants position themselves as reliable and valuable partners in their clients' journey to success. Positive client relationships lead to repeat business, referrals, and lasting impact, solidifying the consultant's position as a trusted advisor in the AI consulting space.

Chapter 10: Ethical and Legal Considerations

AI consulting comes with a profound responsibility to address biases, uphold ethical principles, and navigate complex legal and regulatory frameworks. Chapter 10 delves into the critical topics of addressing bias and fairness in AI, ensuring ethical AI practices, and navigating the legal and regulatory landscape. As AI consultants, understanding these aspects is vital for building AI solutions that are not only technically sound but also equitable, transparent, and compliant. Let's explore the first three topics covered in this chapter:

10.1 Addressing Bias and Fairness in AI:

Bias in AI models can lead to unfair outcomes and perpetuate societal disparities. In this section, we explore the sources of bias in AI data and algorithms. AI consultants learn techniques to identify, measure, and mitigate bias in AI models. We also discuss the importance of diverse and representative datasets and the implications of fairness-aware learning in AI consulting. By addressing bias and promoting fairness, AI consultants strive to deliver AI solutions that treat all individuals equitably.

10.2 Ensuring Ethical AI Practices:

Ethical considerations are at the core of responsible AI consulting. In this section, we delve into ethical guidelines and principles that AI consultants must adhere to during the entire AI development lifecycle. Consultants will learn about informed consent, transparency, accountability, and the responsible use of AI technologies. Ethical AI practices ensure that AI solutions align with societal values and do not compromise privacy, autonomy, or human dignity.

10.3 Navigating Legal and Regulatory Frameworks:

The legal and regulatory landscape surrounding AI is evolving rapidly. This section provides an overview of key legal considerations, such as data protection, intellectual property, and liability. AI consultants will learn to navigate industry-specific regulations and adhere to global standards for AI governance. Additionally, we explore strategies for maintaining compliance with evolving laws and guidelines.

Conclusion: Throughout this chapter, we emphasize the importance of continuous evaluation and improvement of AI solutions from an ethical and legal standpoint. By proactively addressing bias, promoting fairness, and adhering to legal requirements, AI consultants can build AI solutions that inspire trust and facilitate positive societal impact. As ethical AI practices become a hallmark of AI consulting, consultants play an instrumental role in shaping the future of AI that is transparent, equitable, and responsible.

10.1 Addressing Bias and Fairness in AI

Bias in AI systems is a significant ethical concern that can lead to unfair and discriminatory outcomes. As AI technologies become more prevalent in various domains, it is crucial for AI consultants to proactively address bias and ensure fairness in AI models. This section explores strategies to identify and mitigate bias in AI and promote fairness in the development and deployment of AI solutions.

a) **Understanding Bias in AI:** AI bias refers to the presence of unfair and unjustified prejudices in the data used to train AI models. Bias can emerge from historical data that reflects societal stereotypes, leading the AI system to make discriminatory predictions.

b) **Diverse and Representative Data Collection:** To mitigate bias, AI consultants should ensure that the training data is diverse and representative of the population it aims to serve. Balancing the data with equal representation from different demographic groups helps reduce bias.

c) **Bias Assessment and Measurement:** Perform thorough bias assessments during the development process. Various tools and techniques are available to measure bias, such as disparity impact analysis and fairness-aware evaluation metrics.

d) **Addressing Pre-Existing Bias:** AI consultants should actively work to address pre-existing bias in the training data. This may involve data cleaning, re-sampling, or using algorithms that explicitly account for fairness.

e) **Algorithmic Fairness Techniques:** Employ algorithmic fairness techniques, such as adversarial training, re-weighting, and regularization, to mitigate bias in the model's predictions. These techniques can help ensure that the AI system treats different groups fairly.

f) **Interpretability and Explainability:** Using interpretable AI models allows consultants to understand how the model arrives at its decisions. This transparency enables the identification of bias and provides insights into how to address it effectively.

g) **Continuous Monitoring and Model Updating:** AI models should be continuously monitored post-deployment to detect and address any bias that may emerge during real-world usage. Regular model updates can help improve fairness as new data becomes available.

h) **Involving Diverse Stakeholders:** Include diverse stakeholders, such as domain experts and representatives from affected communities, in the AI development process. Their perspectives can provide valuable insights to ensure fairness.

i) **Ethical Review Boards:** Consider setting up ethical review boards or committees that oversee the AI development process. These boards can provide guidance on ethical considerations and flag potential issues related to bias and fairness.

j) **Public Accountability and Transparency:** Promote transparency and public accountability in AI development. Communicate openly about the steps taken to address bias and ensure fairness in AI systems.

Conclusion: Addressing bias and promoting fairness in AI is a critical responsibility for AI consultants. By understanding the nature of bias in AI, collecting diverse and representative data, and employing algorithmic fairness techniques, consultants can reduce bias and improve the fairness of AI models. Regular monitoring, interpretability, and involving diverse stakeholders contribute to the ongoing commitment to fairness. With a focus on ethical considerations and public transparency, AI consultants can develop and deploy AI solutions that not only deliver accurate results but also uphold ethical standards and promote fairness in society.

10.2 Ensuring Ethical AI Practices

Ethical AI practices are essential for building trust, maintaining public confidence, and avoiding harmful consequences associated with AI technologies. AI consultants have a responsibility to uphold ethical principles in all stages of AI development and deployment. In this section, we explore strategies to ensure ethical AI practices in AI consulting.

a) **Define Ethical Guidelines:** Establish clear and comprehensive ethical guidelines that guide AI development and deployment. These guidelines should cover data collection, model training, decision-making processes, and potential societal impacts.

b) **Involve Ethical Experts:** Include ethicists and experts in the development process to provide insights into potential ethical implications and challenges. Collaboration with ethicists ensures a balanced perspective in addressing ethical issues.

c) **Promote Diversity and Inclusion:** Foster diversity and inclusion in AI teams. A diverse team can better understand the needs and concerns of diverse user groups, leading to more inclusive AI solutions.

d) **Conduct Impact Assessments:** Perform comprehensive impact assessments to identify potential ethical risks and consequences associated with AI solutions. Consider the implications on different communities and vulnerable populations.

e) **Prioritize Data Privacy:** Respect user privacy and protect personal data throughout the AI lifecycle. Ensure compliance with relevant data protection regulations and maintain the confidentiality of sensitive information.

f) **Transparent Communication:** Communicate openly with clients and end-users about the ethical considerations in AI solutions. Be transparent about the potential limitations and biases in the models.

g) **Address Bias and Fairness:** Mitigate bias and promote fairness in AI models. Use techniques such as bias assessment, fairness-aware algorithms, and diverse data collection to address potential biases.

h) **Establish Governance Mechanisms:** Implement governance mechanisms to ensure adherence to ethical guidelines. Set up ethical review boards or committees to assess and oversee AI projects.

i) **Continuous Monitoring:** Regularly monitor AI systems to detect and address ethical concerns that may arise during deployment. Continuously improve and update the AI model to align with changing ethical standards.

j) **Engage in Public Discourse:** Participate in public discussions about AI ethics and engage in dialogues with stakeholders, policymakers, and the public to promote responsible AI practices.

k) **Empower Users:** Empower end-users to make informed decisions about AI usage. Provide clear explanations of how AI systems work, their limitations, and the implications of using them.

l) **Commitment to Continuous Learning:** Stay informed about the latest developments in AI ethics and best practices. Commit to ongoing learning and improvement in ethical AI practices.

Conclusion:

Ensuring ethical AI practices is a fundamental responsibility of AI consultants. By defining ethical guidelines, involving ethical experts, and promoting diversity, consultants can address ethical concerns proactively. Impact assessments, data privacy, and transparent communication build trust and accountability. Addressing bias and fairness, establishing governance mechanisms, and continuous monitoring contribute to the ethical development and deployment of AI solutions. Engaging in public discourse and empowering users demonstrate a commitment to responsible AI practices. By upholding ethical principles, AI consultants make a positive impact on society and contribute to the ethical advancement of AI technologies.

10.3 Navigating Legal and Regulatory Frameworks

In AI consulting, compliance with legal and regulatory frameworks is crucial to ensure ethical and responsible use of AI technologies. AI consultants must be well-versed in the laws and regulations that govern AI applications in different domains. Navigating these frameworks effectively helps avoid legal liabilities, protect user rights, and build trust with clients. In this section, we explore strategies to navigate legal and regulatory frameworks in AI consulting.

a) **Understand Applicable Laws and Regulations:** AI consultants must familiarize themselves with relevant laws and regulations governing AI, data privacy, intellectual property, and industry-specific guidelines. Stay up-to-date with changes in regulations that may impact AI projects.

b) **Work with Legal Experts:** Collaborate with legal experts who specialize in AI and technology-related laws. Legal experts can provide guidance on compliance and risk management.

c) **Conduct Legal Assessments:** Conduct legal assessments to identify potential legal risks associated with AI projects. Assess how AI solutions may impact user rights, data usage, and compliance with relevant regulations.

d) **Obtain Informed Consent:** In situations where data collection or AI usage requires informed consent, ensure that clients and end-users provide explicit and informed consent for the intended purposes.

e) **Protect Intellectual Property:** Understand intellectual property rights related to AI models, algorithms, and related technologies. Establish ownership and licensing agreements with clients to protect intellectual property rights.

f) **Compliance with Data Protection Laws:** Adhere to data protection laws, such as GDPR, HIPAA, or CCPA, when collecting, storing, and processing data. Implement privacy safeguards and obtain consent where necessary.

g) **Assess AI Bias and Fairness:** Consider potential legal implications of AI bias and fairness. Ensure that AI models do not lead to discriminatory outcomes, as this may raise legal concerns.

h) **Monitor AI Performance and Compliance:** Continuously monitor AI solutions to ensure they comply with legal and regulatory requirements. Regularly audit models for fairness and bias to address potential legal risks.

i) **Develop Ethical AI Policies:** Incorporate ethical AI policies into the consulting process to align with legal and regulatory expectations. Establish guidelines that promote responsible AI practices.

j) **Collaborate with Clients on Compliance:** Work closely with clients to ensure that AI solutions align with their legal and regulatory obligations. Provide necessary information and support to help clients comply with relevant laws.

k) **Establish Risk Mitigation Strategies:** Develop risk mitigation strategies to handle legal challenges that may arise during AI deployment. Be prepared to respond to potential legal disputes proactively.

l) **Document Compliance Efforts:** Maintain comprehensive documentation of compliance efforts, including legal assessments, consent forms, and risk management strategies. Proper documentation helps demonstrate due diligence and accountability.

Conclusion:

Navigating legal and regulatory frameworks is an essential aspect of AI consulting. By understanding applicable laws, working with legal experts, and conducting legal assessments, consultants can navigate legal complexities effectively. Ensuring compliance with data protection laws, intellectual property rights, and ethical guidelines promotes responsible AI practices. Regular monitoring, risk mitigation, and collaboration with clients on compliance contribute to successful AI projects while mitigating legal risks. By prioritizing legal and regulatory compliance, AI consultants uphold ethical standards and build trust with clients and users.

Chapter 11: Staying Updated in the Dynamic AI Landscape

In the ever-evolving landscape of AI consulting, continuous learning and staying updated with the latest trends are imperative for success. Chapter 11 explores the significance of continuous learning, networking in AI communities, and staying informed about cutting-edge AI trends. As AI consultants, embracing a growth mindset and staying at the forefront of advancements are key to delivering innovative and transformative AI solutions. Let's explore the first three topics covered in this chapter:

11.1 Continuous Learning and Skill Enhancement:

AI technologies and methodologies are constantly evolving. In this section, we emphasize the importance of ongoing learning to keep up with the latest advancements in AI. AI consultants will discover various resources for continuous learning, such as online courses, workshops, research papers, and AI conferences. Additionally, we discuss the value of interdisciplinary learning to expand problem-solving abilities and creativity.

11.2 Networking and Engaging in AI Communities:

Networking within AI communities offers invaluable opportunities for knowledge sharing, collaboration, and professional growth. In this section, we explore various AI communities, forums, and social media platforms where AI consultants can connect with peers, researchers, and industry experts. Consultants will learn to leverage these networks to seek guidance, share experiences, and participate in AI-related discussions and projects.

11.3 Staying Informed About Latest AI Trends:

In the fast-paced world of AI, staying informed about the latest trends and breakthroughs is essential. This section covers strategies for staying up-to-date with AI news, publications, and research from leading institutions and organizations. We also discuss the significance of monitoring AI applications across diverse industries to gain insights into emerging use cases and innovative solutions.

Conclusion: Throughout this chapter, we emphasize the intrinsic link between continuous learning and professional growth. AI consultants who embrace lifelong learning are better equipped to address novel challenges and deliver pioneering AI solutions. Engaging with AI communities fosters a collaborative environment where consultants can learn from each other's experiences and contribute to the advancement of AI knowledge. By actively staying informed about the latest AI trends, consultants maintain their competitive edge and continue to drive innovation and excellence in AI consulting.

11.1 Continuous Learning and Skill Enhancement

In the dynamic and ever-evolving field of AI, continuous learning and skill enhancement are not just advantageous but essential for AI consultants. As technology advances and new methodologies emerge, staying up-to-date is crucial to provide cutting-edge solutions, remain competitive, and deliver maximum value to clients. This section explores the importance of continuous learning and strategies for skill enhancement in AI consulting.

Importance of Continuous Learning:

a) **Keeping Up with Advancements:** AI is a rapidly progressing field with frequent breakthroughs and innovations. Continuous learning allows consultants to stay current with the latest advancements and best practices.

b) **Adapting to Changing Trends:** The AI landscape is influenced by changing trends, such as the popularity of different algorithms or the emergence of new tools. Continuous learning helps consultants adapt to these shifts effectively.

c) **Enhancing Problem-Solving Skills:** AI consultants encounter diverse challenges in their projects. Continuous learning expands their problem-solving skills, enabling them to approach new tasks with a versatile mindset.

d) **Embracing Ethical AI Practices:** AI consultants must navigate ethical considerations. Continuous learning helps them stay informed about ethical frameworks and ensures responsible AI development and deployment.

Strategies for Skill Enhancement:

a) **Enroll in AI Courses and Certifications:** Online platforms and institutions offer a wide range of AI courses and certifications. Enroll in reputable programs to acquire new skills and validate expertise.

b) **Attend Workshops and Webinars:** Participate in workshops and webinars conducted by industry experts to learn about the latest trends, techniques, and case studies in AI.

c) **Engage in Practical Projects:** Hands-on experience is invaluable. Engage in practical AI projects to gain real-world insights and develop proficiency in AI tools and technologies.

d) **Collaborate on AI Research:** Collaborate with academic institutions or researchers to work on AI research projects. Research involvement sharpens analytical skills and fosters a deeper understanding of AI theories.

e) **Participate in AI Competitions:** AI competitions and hackathons offer opportunities to solve complex problems and compete with peers, honing critical thinking and innovative skills.

f) **Join AI Special Interest Groups:** Join AI special interest groups or communities to connect with like-minded professionals and participate in knowledge-sharing activities.

g) **Follow Thought Leaders and Blogs:** Follow renowned AI thought leaders and read AI-related blogs to gain insights into emerging trends, research findings, and expert opinions.

h) **Pursue Multidisciplinary Learning:** AI intersects with various fields like neuroscience, psychology, and economics. Pursue multidisciplinary learning to explore diverse perspectives and enhance problem-solving

i) **Seek Feedback and Mentorship:** Seek feedback on your AI projects and seek mentorship from experienced professionals. Constructive criticism and guidance facilitate growth and improvement.

j) **Document and Reflect:** Document your learning journey and reflect on progress regularly. Reviewing past projects and challenges helps identify areas for improvement.

Conclusion: Continuous learning and skill enhancement are at the core of successful AI consulting. By staying updated with advancements, embracing ethical AI practices, and adapting to changing trends, consultants thrive in the dynamic AI landscape. Enrolling in courses, attending workshops, and collaborating on research foster skill development. Engaging in practical projects and competitions hones problem-solving abilities. Following thought leaders and seeking mentorship provide valuable guidance. The dedication to continuous learning ensures that AI consultants consistently deliver innovative and impactful solutions, making a positive difference in the AI industry and beyond.

11.2 Networking and Engaging in AI Communities

Networking and active engagement in AI communities are integral components of a successful AI consulting career. Building connections with like-minded professionals, researchers, and enthusiasts not only enhances knowledge sharing but also opens doors to new opportunities, collaborations, and insights. In this section, we explore the importance of networking and strategies for effective engagement in AI communities.

Importance of Networking:

a) **Knowledge Sharing:** Networking allows AI consultants to exchange knowledge, experiences, and best practices with others in the field. It fosters a collaborative learning environment.

b) **Professional Development:** Engaging with peers and experts can lead to mentorship opportunities, workshops, and conferences that contribute to ongoing professional development.

c) **Stay Updated:** Networking keeps consultants informed about the latest advancements, trends, and breakthroughs in AI, helping them remain at the cutting edge of the field.

d) **Access to Resources:** Being part of a community provides access to valuable resources like research papers, tools, and libraries that facilitate learning and project development.

e) **Collaboration Opportunities:** Networking opens doors to potential collaborations on research projects, AI initiatives, and joint ventures, expanding consultants' horizons.

Strategies for Effective Networking:

a) **Join Online AI Platforms:** Participate in AI-focused forums, social media groups, and professional networking platforms to connect with AI professionals worldwide.

b) **Attend AI Conferences and Meetups:** Attend conferences, seminars, and local AI meetups to meet experts, share ideas, and forge connections in person.

c) **Engage in Open Source Projects:** Contribute to open-source AI projects and interact with the developer community to showcase expertise and gain recognition.

d) **Participate in Webinars and Workshops:** Join webinars and workshops conducted by AI thought leaders and organizations to network and learn from industry experts.

e) **Create a Personal Brand:** Establish a strong online presence through a personal website, blog, or social media. Demonstrate expertise and share valuable content with the AI community.

f) **Offer Value to Others:** Share insights, answer questions, and provide assistance to fellow AI enthusiasts. Being helpful fosters goodwill and strengthens connections.

g) **Collaborate on Research Papers:** Collaborate with researchers on AI-related research papers. Co-authoring publications enhances visibility and credibility in the academic community.

h) **Host AI Events and Webinars:** Organize webinars, workshops, or events to share knowledge and attract like-minded professionals to network with.

i) **Join AI Special Interest Groups:** Participate in special interest groups focused on specific AI subfields or industries to connect with professionals with similar interests.

j) **Network at AI Hackathons:** Participate in AI hackathons to solve problems collaboratively, build relationships with team members, and showcase skills.

Conclusion: Networking and engaging in AI communities are integral to professional growth and success in AI consulting. By connecting with experts, sharing knowledge, and staying updated with the latest trends, consultants remain at the forefront of the dynamic AI landscape. Participating in conferences, webinars, and local meetups allows consultants to build meaningful connections and access valuable resources. Contributing to open-source projects and collaborating on research papers further enhances visibility and recognition. By offering value, sharing insights, and actively participating in AI communities, consultants enrich their professional journey, paving the way for new opportunities, collaborations, and an expanded skillset.

11.3 Staying Informed About Latest AI Trends

In the rapidly evolving field of artificial intelligence (AI), staying informed about the latest trends is crucial for AI consultants. Being aware of emerging technologies, research breakthroughs, and industry developments allows consultants to make informed decisions, provide cutting-edge solutions, and remain competitive in the AI landscape. This section explores the importance of staying informed about AI trends and strategies to do so effectively.

Importance of Staying Informed:

Identifying New Opportunities. Being aware of emerging AI trends helps consultants identify new business opportunities and potential applications of AI in different industries.

a) **Enhancing Decision-Making:** Informed decisions are essential for successful AI projects. Knowing the latest trends empowers consultants to choose the most appropriate tools and techniques for specific tasks.

b) **Improving Client Solutions:** Staying informed allows consultants to implement the most recent AI methodologies, resulting in more effective and efficient solutions for their clients.

c) **Keeping Up with Competitors:** The AI field is highly competitive. Being up-to-date with trends ensures that consultants can stay ahead of competitors and offer unique value to their clients.

d) **Contributing to Thought Leadership:** Consultants who are well-informed about AI trends can become thought leaders in the industry, sharing valuable insights and perspectives with the AI community.

Strategies for Staying Informed:

a) **Follow AI News Websites:** Regularly follow reputable AI news websites and tech publications that cover the latest trends, research, and breakthroughs in the AI field.

b) **Subscribe to AI Journals and Newsletters:** Subscribe to academic journals, research papers, and AI-focused newsletters to receive updates on recent studies and advancements.

c) **Attend AI Conferences and Webinars:** Participate in AI conferences, webinars, and virtual events to hear from experts, learn about the latest trends, and network with professionals in the field.

d) **Join AI Groups on Social Media:** Be part of AI-focused groups and communities on platforms like LinkedIn, Twitter, and Reddit to engage in discussions and share knowledge with peers.

e) **Follow AI Thought Leaders:** Follow AI thought leaders, researchers, and practitioners on social media platforms to access their insights and learn from their expertise.

f) **Engage in Research Papers:** Read research papers and publications in the AI domain to gain in-depth knowledge about the latest advancements and methodologies.

g) **Experiment with AI Tools:** Continuously experiment with new AI tools, libraries, and platforms to understand their capabilities and how they can enhance AI solutions.

h) **Collaborate with AI Researchers:** Collaborate with academic institutions or researchers on AI-related projects to gain exposure to cutting-edge research and trends.

i) **Participate in AI Competitions:** Join AI competitions and hackathons to tackle real-world challenges and learn from the diverse approaches of other participants.

j) **Engage with AI Communities:** Engage in AI communities, forums, and discussion platforms to share insights and learn from the experiences of other AI enthusiasts.

Conclusion: Staying informed about the latest AI trends is paramount for AI consultants seeking to excel in their field. Regularly following AI news, subscribing to academic journals, and attending conferences provide a wealth of information on the latest advancements and industry developments. Engaging with thought leaders, experimenting with new tools, and participating in AI competitions further enriches knowledge. Active involvement in AI communities fosters continuous learning and networking opportunities. By staying informed, AI consultants can provide innovative solutions, make informed decisions, and position themselves as valuable contributors to the dynamic world of artificial intelligence.Sample AI Consulting Project Case Studies

AI consulting project case studies:

To gain a better understanding of how AI consultants tackle real-world challenges, let's explore some sample AI consulting project case studies:

Case Study 1: Predictive Maintenance for Manufacturing

Client: A large manufacturing company

Challenge: The client's production line faced frequent breakdowns, causing costly downtimes and maintenance expenses. They sought a solution to predict machine failures in advance to optimize maintenance schedules and reduce unplanned downtime.

Solution: The AI consultant designed a predictive maintenance system using machine learning. They collected historical sensor data from the machines and employed an anomaly detection algorithm to identify patterns indicative of potential failures. The consultant developed a predictive model that provided the probability of machine failure within a given time frame.

Outcome: The predictive maintenance system allowed the client to schedule maintenance before critical failures occurred. This resulted in a significant reduction in unplanned downtime, leading to improved operational efficiency and cost savings.

Case Study 2: Sentiment Analysis for Customer Feedback

Client: An e-commerce company

Challenge: The client received a large volume of customer feedback in various forms, such as product reviews, emails, and social media comments. They needed a way to analyze this unstructured data to gain insights into customer sentiment and identify areas for improvement.

Solution: The AI consultant implemented natural language processing (NLP) techniques to perform sentiment analysis on the customer feedback data. They trained a sentiment analysis model using machine learning to classify feedback as positive, negative, or neutral.

Outcome: The client gained valuable insights into customer sentiment, allowing them to identify recurring issues, address customer concerns promptly, and make data-driven decisions to improve their products and services.

Case Study 3: Personalized Healthcare Recommendations

Client: A healthcare provider

Challenge: The client wanted to improve patient outcomes by providing personalized treatment recommendations. They sought to leverage patient data, medical history, and research findings to create personalized treatment plans for various conditions.

Solution: The AI consultant developed a personalized healthcare recommendation system using a combination of machine learning and patient data analysis. They utilized patient electronic health records (EHRs) and clinical data to build patient profiles. The consultant then used collaborative filtering and content-based filtering techniques to match patients with similar characteristics and treatment responses. This allowed for the creation of tailored treatment plans for each patient.

Outcome: The personalized healthcare recommendation system led to improved patient outcomes, reduced treatment trial-and-error, and enhanced patient satisfaction. It also allowed the healthcare provider to optimize resource allocation and treatment protocols.

Case Study 4: Fraud Detection for Financial Institution

Client: A financial institution

Challenge: The client faced challenges in detecting fraudulent transactions in real-time. They needed an AI-powered fraud detection system to identify suspicious activities and prevent fraudulent transactions.

Solution: The AI consultant developed a fraud detection system using machine learning algorithms. They used historical transaction data, including legitimate and fraudulent transactions, to train the model. The system utilized anomaly detection and pattern recognition to identify unusual transaction patterns in real-time.

Outcome: The fraud detection system significantly reduced false positives and false negatives, improving the overall accuracy of detecting fraudulent transactions. This led to enhanced security, reduced financial losses, and increased customer trust in the financial institution.

Each of these case studies showcases the diverse applications of AI consulting across different industries. AI consultants leverage their technical expertise and problem-solving skills to deliver impactful solutions that address unique challenges faced by their clients. From predictive maintenance in manufacturing to sentiment analysis in e-commerce and personalized healthcare recommendations, AI consulting projects have the potential to drive positive change and optimize operations across various sectors.

Conclusion: Becoming an AI consultant is an exciting journey that demands a combination of technical expertise, problem-solving skills, ethical awareness, and continuous learning. This book has explored the various aspects of becoming an AI consultant, providing a comprehensive guide to navigating this dynamic and rewarding career path.

Reflecting on Your Journey to Becoming an AI Consultant

As you come to the end of this book on "AI Consulting 101," take a moment to reflect on your journey and the insights you have gained along the way. Embarking on a career as an AI consultant is a rewarding and challenging path that requires dedication, passion, and a commitment to continuous growth. Consider the following points as you reflect on your journey:

a) **Discovery of Interest:** What sparked your interest in AI consulting? Was it a fascination with cutting-edge technologies, a desire to solve complex problems, or the potential to make a positive impact on businesses and society? Understanding the initial motivations that led you to this field can help you stay focused and passionate in your career.

b) **Learning and Skill Development:** Reflect on the skills and knowledge you have acquired throughout this journey. How have you expanded your technical expertise in AI, data management, programming languages, and model development? Celebrate the progress you have made and identify areas where you can continue to grow.

c) **Challenges and Breakthroughs:** Consider the challenges you encountered during your journey. Did you face obstacles in understanding complex AI concepts or in navigating ethical dilemmas? Reflect on the breakthroughs and strategies that helped you overcome these challenges, as they can serve as valuable lessons for future endeavors.

d) **Real-Life Applications:** Think about the real-life AI use cases and projects you explored during your learning process. How have these examples shaped your understanding of

AI's potential applications across various industries? Consider how these insights can inform your future consulting projects.

e) **Ethical Awareness:** As an AI consultant, you play a crucial role in shaping ethical AI practices. How has your awareness of bias, fairness, and data privacy evolved? Consider how you will uphold ethical considerations in your work to ensure responsible AI solutions.

f) **Networking and Engagement:** Reflect on the connections you have made with AI professionals, researchers, and thought leaders. Have you actively engaged in AI communities and shared your knowledge with others? Networking provides opportunities for collaboration and continued learning.

g) **Continuous Learning:** Embrace the idea that learning is a lifelong journey. How will you stay proactive in staying informed about the latest AI trends and advancements? Reflect on the strategies you plan to implement to continue growing as an AI consultant.

h) **Future Aspirations:** As you reflect on your journey, consider your future aspirations as an AI consultant. What are your short-term and long-term goals? How will you leverage your skills and expertise to make a meaningful impact on businesses and society?

Remember that the path to becoming an AI consultant is not just about reaching a destination; it's about embracing a mindset of continuous learning, adaptability, and a commitment to ethical and responsible AI practices. By reflecting on your journey, you gain valuable insights that can guide you as you embark on an exciting and fulfilling career in AI consulting. Stay curious, stay determined, and always embrace the possibilities that AI presents in shaping a better future.

Words of Advice from Experienced AI Consultants

As you embark on your journey to becoming an AI consultant, it is valuable to learn from the experiences and wisdom of those who have already succeeded in this field. Here are some words of advice from experienced AI consultants to guide you on your path:

a) **Embrace Lifelong Learning:** The field of AI is constantly evolving, and new technologies and methodologies emerge rapidly. Never stop learning and stay curious. Continuous learning is essential to stay relevant and provide innovative solutions to your clients.

b) **Focus on Problem-Solving:** AI is a powerful tool, but it is essential to focus on solving real-world problems for your clients. Understand their unique challenges and use AI to deliver practical and impactful solutions.

c) **Build Strong Foundations:** Develop a solid understanding of the fundamentals of AI, including mathematics, statistics, and programming. A strong foundation will serve as a springboard for your AI consulting career.

d) **Network and Collaborate:** Engage with the AI community and build relationships with fellow professionals, researchers, and thought leaders. Collaboration can lead to exciting opportunities and expand your knowledge base.

e) **Prioritize Ethics and Fairness:** Ethical considerations should be at the core of every AI project. Ensure fairness, transparency, and privacy in your solutions, and be mindful of the potential biases that AI models may exhibit.

f) **Gain Hands-On Experience:** Theory is essential, but practical experience is invaluable. Engage in AI projects, experiment with AI tools, and work on real-world datasets to sharpen your skills and understand the nuances of AI implementation.

g) **Communicate Effectively:** AI consulting involves working closely with clients and stakeholders who may not have technical expertise. Learn to communicate complex AI concepts in a clear and accessible manner to facilitate effective collaboration.

h) **Stay Humble and Open-Minded:** The AI field is vast and multidisciplinary. Stay humble and open-minded, and be willing to learn from others. Embrace diverse perspectives to enrich your problem-solving approaches.

i) **Be Adaptable:** The AI landscape can change rapidly, and projects may face unexpected challenges. Be adaptable and ready to pivot your strategies when needed to achieve the best outcomes.

j) **Celebrate Successes and Learn from Failures:** Celebrate your achievements and successes, no matter how small. At the same time, don't fear failures; view them as opportunities for growth and learning.

k) **Promote Responsible AI:** As an AI consultant, you have a responsibility to advocate for responsible AI practices. Ensure that AI technologies are used ethically and that their potential impacts are thoroughly assessed.

l) **Stay Passionate:** Passion is the driving force behind excellence. Stay passionate about AI and its transformative potential. Let your passion fuel your dedication to making a positive impact through your work.

Remember that every AI consultant's journey is unique, and there is no one-size-fits-all approach to success. Embrace challenges, stay committed to learning, and maintain a genuine passion for the work you do. Your journey as an AI consultant will be marked by growth, learning, and the satisfaction of contributing to the advancement of AI technologies for the betterment of society.

Appendix:

Glossary of AI Terminology

As you delve into the world of artificial intelligence (AI), you'll encounter various technical terms and concepts. This glossary provides concise definitions of common AI terminology to aid your understanding:

Artificial Intelligence (AI): The simulation of human intelligence in machines, enabling them to perform tasks that typically require human intelligence, such as learning, reasoning, problem-solving, and decision-making.

Machine Learning (ML): A subset of AI that involves the development of algorithms and models that enable computers to learn from and make predictions or decisions based on data, without being explicitly programmed.

Deep Learning: A specialized form of machine learning that involves the use of artificial neural networks to enable computers to learn from vast amounts of unstructured data and perform complex tasks.

Natural Language Processing (NLP): A branch of AI that focuses on enabling machines to understand, interpret, and interact with human language in a way that is both meaningful and contextually relevant.

Data Science: The process of extracting knowledge and insights from structured and unstructured data using various statistical, mathematical, and machine learning techniques.

Supervised Learning: A type of machine learning where the algorithm is trained on labeled data, meaning it is provided with input-output pairs to learn from and can make predictions on new, unseen data.

Unsupervised Learning: A type of machine learning where the algorithm is trained on unlabeled data, and it attempts to find patterns, structures, or representations within the data without specific guidance.

Reinforcement Learning: A type of machine learning where an algorithm learns through trial and error by interacting with an environment and receiving feedback in the form of rewards or penalties.

Algorithm: A set of rules or procedures followed by a computer to solve a specific problem or perform a particular task.

Artificial Neural Network (ANN): A computational model inspired by the human brain's neural network, used in deep learning to process and learn from complex data.

Feature Engineering: The process of selecting, transforming, and extracting relevant features from raw data to improve the performance of machine learning algorithms.

Bias: A systematic error introduced into the model due to the representation of the data or the algorithm's design, leading to unfair or discriminatory outcomes.

Fairness: Ensuring that AI systems treat all individuals or groups fairly and without bias, regardless of their characteristics or background.

Data Privacy: The protection of individuals' personal and sensitive information in data collection, storage, and processing to maintain confidentiality and comply with data protection regulations.

Overfitting: A situation in machine learning where a model performs well on the training data but poorly on unseen data due to its inability to generalize.

Underfitting: A situation in machine learning where a model fails to capture the underlying patterns in the data, leading to poor performance on both training and unseen data.

Deployment: The process of integrating a trained AI model into a production environment to make real-world predictions or decisions.

Hyperparameter: A parameter that is set before the training process begins and influences the model's learning process, such as the learning rate or the number of hidden layers in a neural network.

Big Data: Extremely large and complex datasets that require specialized techniques and technologies for storage, processing, and analysis.

Internet of Things (IoT): The network of interconnected physical devices, vehicles, appliances, and other objects embedded with sensors and software that collect and exchange data over the internet.

Chatbot: An AI-powered software application designed to simulate conversation with human users, often used for customer support and information retrieval.

This glossary provides a starting point to familiarize yourself with essential AI terminology. As you progress in your AI journey, you will encounter many more concepts and terms that will expand your understanding of this fascinating field.

Additional Resources for Further Learning

As you continue your journey to become an AI consultant, there are numerous resources available to deepen your knowledge, expand your skills, and stay updated with the latest developments in the field of artificial intelligence. Here are some valuable resources to explore:

Online Courses and Platforms:

Coursera: Offers a wide range of AI and machine learning courses from top universities and institutions.

edX: Provides AI-related courses and certifications from renowned universities.

Udacity: Offers nanodegree programs on AI and specialized AI topics.

Books:

"Artificial Intelligence: A Modern Approach" by Stuart Russell and Peter Norvig.

"Hands-On Machine Learning with Scikit-Learn, Keras, and TensorFlow" by Aurélien Géron.

"Deep Learning" by Ian Goodfellow, Yoshua Bengio, and Aaron Courville.

AI Research Journals and Publications:

arXiv.org: A repository of research papers in various AI subfields, such as machine learning, NLP, and computer vision.

AI Journal: An academic journal covering AI research and applications.

AI Conferences and Events:

NeurIPS (Conference on Neural Information Processing Systems): An annual machine learning and computational neuroscience conference.

CVPR (Conference on Computer Vision and Pattern Recognition): A premier computer vision conference.

AI Research Institutions and Blogs:

OpenAI Blog: Features articles on AI research and developments from the OpenAI team.

Google AI Blog: Provides insights into AI projects and research conducted at Google.

AI Ethics and Responsible AI:

AI Ethics Guidelines and Frameworks: Explore resources from organizations like the IEEE and the Future of Life Institute.

Partnership on AI: A collaborative platform addressing AI's societal challenges.

AI Competitions and Challenges:

Kaggle: A platform for AI competitions, datasets, and forums for knowledge exchange.

AIcrowd: Hosts various AI challenges and hackathons.

AI Podcasts and Videos:

"The AI Podcast" by NVIDIA: Features interviews and discussions with AI experts.

"Lex Fridman Podcast": Delves into AI, machine learning, and other science and technology topics.

AI Tool Documentation and GitHub Repositories:

TensorFlow: An open-source machine learning framework by Google.

PyTorch: An open-source machine learning library by Facebook.

AI Meetups and Webinars:

Meetup.com: Find local AI meetups and events to connect with other AI enthusiasts in your area.

Webinars by AI organizations and platforms: Participate in online events to learn from AI experts.

Remember that AI is an interdisciplinary field, and learning from various resources will provide a well-rounded understanding. Continuously exploring new resources and engaging with the AI community will contribute to your growth as an AI consultant.

Lastly, don't forget to follow AI news outlets and subscribe to industry newsletters to stay updated with the latest trends and breakthroughs in artificial intelligence.

The AI landscape is ever-evolving, be knowledgeable.

Printed in Great Britain
by Amazon